CAPE VERDE TRAVEL GUIDE

A Complete Guide for all Including First-Timers to Embark on a Breathtaking Adventure in the Cabo Verde

James D. Vollmer

Copyright © 2023 by James D. Vollmer

All rights reserved. No part of this publication may be reproduced, distributed, or transmitted in any form or by any means, including photocopying, recording, or other electronic or mechanical methods, without the prior written permission of the publisher, except in the case of brief quotations embodied in critical reviews and certain other noncommercial uses permitted by copyright law.

For permission requests, contact the publisher.

Disclaimer ⚠

The information provided in this "Iceland Travel Guide" is accurate to the best of the author's knowledge at the time of publication. However, the author and publisher make no representation or warranties with respect to the accuracy or completeness of the contents of this guidebook and specifically disclaim any implied warranties of merchantability or fitness for a particular purpose. The author and publisher shall have no liability to any person or entity with respect to any loss or damage caused or alleged to be caused directly or indirectly by the information contained in this guidebook.

Table of Contents

About This Guide 7
Introduction 9
    Welcome to Cape Verde 9
    Introduction to the Islands 11
    A Glimpse into Cape Verde's History 12
    Understanding the Climate and Geography 13
Discovering Cape Verde 17
    Top 25 Must-Visit Attractions 17
    Pristine Beaches of Cape Verde 23
    Hiking Trails and Natural Wonders 34
    Culinary Delights: A Taste of Cape Verde 44
    Vibrant Nightlife and Entertainment 46
    Cultural Heritage Sites 60
    Enjoying Cape Verde Without Spending a Dime 73
Travel Essentials 79
    Optimal Times to Visit 82
    Navigating Arrival and Transportation 84
    Essential Travel Tips for a Smooth Journey 87
    Annual Events Calendar 90
    10-Day Itineraries for Every Traveler 90

Island by Island: A Comprehensive Guide 97
   Santiago: The Heart of Cape Verde 97
   Sal: A Beach Lover's Paradise 103
   Boa Vista: The Dunes Island 110
   Fogo: The Island of Fire 117
   São Vicente: The Cultural Hub 124

Embracing the Culture 131
   The Rhythms of Cape Verdean Music 131
   Savoring the Local Cuisine 133
   Celebrating Festivals and Traditions 135
   Dress and Etiquette: Tips for Respectful Interactions 137

Practical Information for Travelers 141
   Finding the Perfect Accommodation 141
   Health and Safety Guidelines 143
   Understanding Local Laws and Customs 146
   Staying Connected: Communication Tips 148
   Some Common Portuguese Phrases 148

Cape Verde Today 151
   Leadership and Governance: The Role of the President 151
   Economic Insights and Recent Achievements 153

Conclusion 157

Recommendations 158

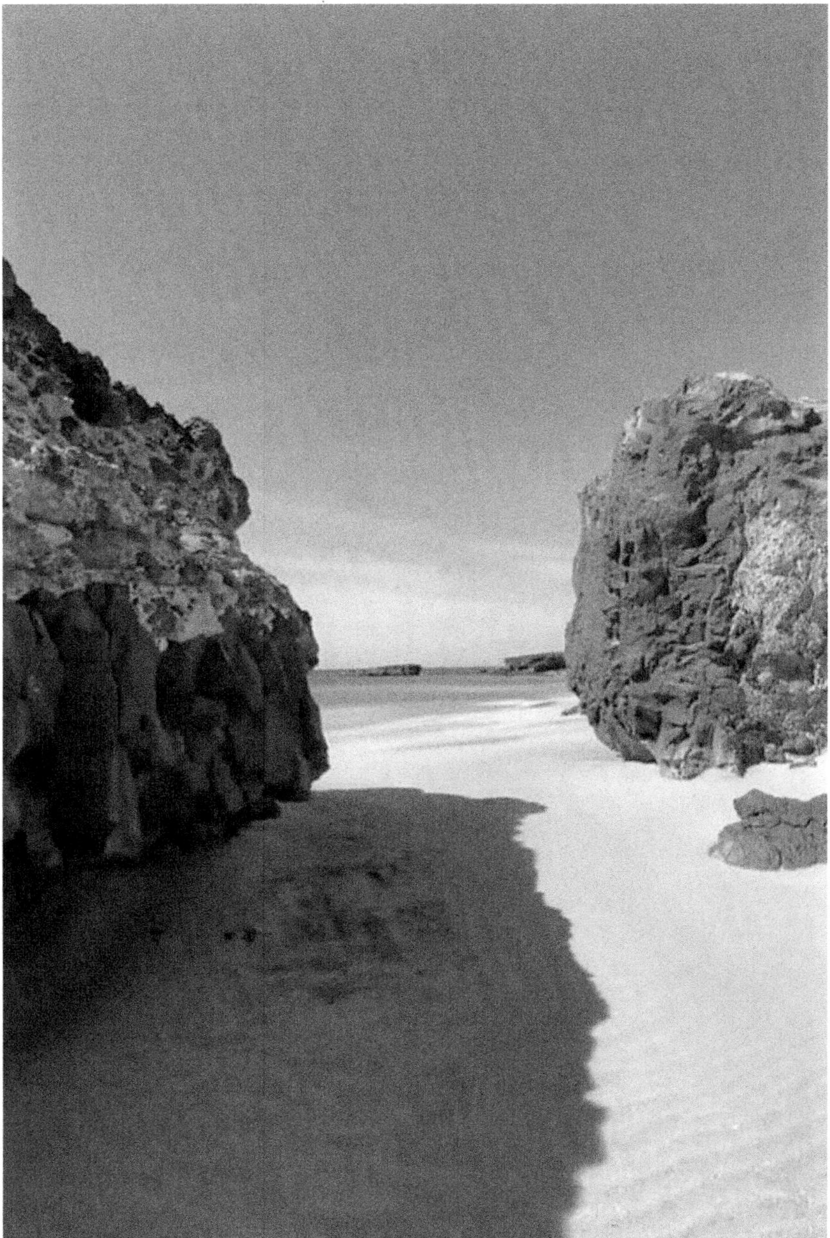

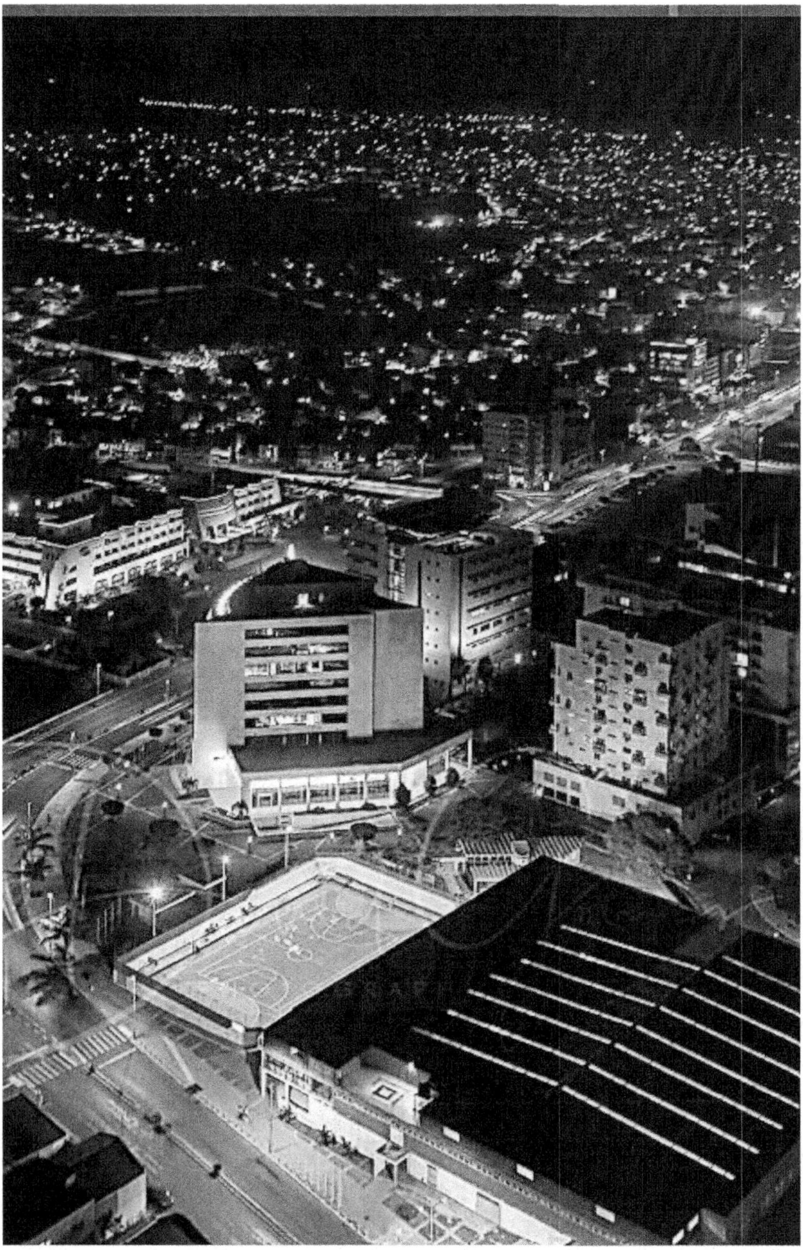

About This Guide

Welcome aboard the journey with "Cape Verde Travel Guide 2024," the perfect partner for diving into the heart of Cape Verde's magical isles. Tailored for every type of explorer - be it solo wanderers, lovebirds on a quest for romance, families in pursuit of unforgettable tales, or a squad eager for new thrills - our guide aims to arm you with all you need to uncover the splendors of this dazzling archipelago.

Purpose of the Guide
At the heart of this guide lies a simple mission: to paint a vivid picture of Cape Verde, showcasing its breathtaking landscapes, vibrant culture, and unparalleled attractions. We've poured over details to ensure you get a holistic view of what awaits. From sun-kissed beaches to lively festivals, from exquisite local dishes to thrilling outdoor adventures, we've got every corner covered.

How to Use This Guide
Crafted for ease and accessibility, the guide unfolds chapter by chapter, each focusing on a different slice of Cape Verdean travel. Looking for accommodation tips, gastronomic recommendations, or transport advice? It's all here, meticulously detailed to help you sketch out your journey and make choices with confidence.

We suggest giving the guide a read before setting off, to get a grip on the essentials and sort out your must-dos. And once you're there, let this guide be your trusty sidekick to steer through the islands and soak in the essence of Cape Verde.

Feedback and Updates
The realm of travel is always on the move, and so are we, striving to keep this guide spot-on and reliable. Your insights and updates are gold to us, aiding in refining future versions. Got a tip or spotted a snag? We're all ears.

Don't forget to swing by our website for the freshest updates and extra nuggets of wisdom to spice up your Cape Verde adventure.

Enjoy Your Journey
Cape Verde beckons with promises of discovery, tranquility, and cultural awakening. With this guide as your navigator, we hope you're geared up and thrilled to chart the wonders of the islands. Dive into the local lifestyle, marvel at nature's masterpieces, and gather stories to cherish.

Thanks for picking "Cape Verde Travel Guide 2024" as your travel ally. Here's to a journey that's safe, joyful, and brimming with discoveries in Cape Verde!

Introduction

Welcome to Cape Verde

Welcome to the enchanting shores of Cape Verde, nestled off Africa's northwest coast, where the promise of untouched beaches, a vibrant cultural scene, and unparalleled hospitality beckons. Known to its residents as Cabo Verde, this archipelago is a rich blend of African, Portuguese, and Brazilian essences, offering an unforgettable journey.

Discover the Islands

Cape Verde unfolds across ten main islands and numerous islets, each boasting its unique allure. From Sal and Boa Vista's golden beaches to Fogo's dramatic volcanic scenery, the archipelago invites you to discover its diverse natural wonders. Whether your heart yearns for adventure, serenity, or a deep dive into culture, Cape Verde welcomes you with open arms.

A Rich Cultural Tapestry

At the heart of Cape Verde beats a rhythm fueled by Morna, Funaná, and Coladeira, music genres that weave through the fabric of local life, charming both islanders and visitors. The islands come alive with vivid festivals like Mindelo's Carnival and São João Baptista's festivities, a testament to the vibrant spirit and rich traditions of its people.

Culinary Delights

The flavors of Cape Verde are as diverse as its landscapes, a delectable fusion of African, Portuguese, and Brazilian influences. Seafood reigns supreme, with dishes like cachupa and grilled lobster offering a taste of the ocean's bounty. The sweetness of papaya and mango complements the culinary adventure, adding a tropical zest.

Warm Hospitality

Perhaps the most enduring memory of Cape Verde is the warmth with which its people embrace visitors. The concept of "morabeza" encapsulates this open-heartedness, ensuring a stay that feels as comforting as home.

Sustainable Travel

With a keen commitment to preserving its pristine environment, Cape Verde champions sustainable tourism. Visitors are encouraged to tread lightly, embracing the local culture and natural beauty in a way that ensures their preservation for future adventurers.

Your Adventure Awaits

As you set sail for Cape Verde, let the islands enchant you with their beauty, cultural richness, and the warmth of their people. Whether scaling volcanic heights, swaying to local rhythms, or basking on sunlit shores, an unforgettable adventure awaits.

Welcome to Cape Verde, where your island dream sets sail!

Introduction to the Islands

Oh, the charm of Cape Verde, a cluster of ten unique islands and a sprinkle of islets, floating in the Atlantic, off West Africa's coast. It's a world where every isle tells its own story, painting a panorama of varied landscapes and adventures for those who wander.

Take Santiago, the archipelago's giant, cradling Praia, the bustling capital. Here, African and Portuguese threads weave a rich cultural tapestry. Venture inland, and you'll find mountains guarding green valleys and thriving plantations, while the coast whispers tales of sandy shores and quaint fishing hamlets.

Then there's **Sal**, where the sands are as white as dreams and the waters a clear, mesmerizing turquoise. It's a paradise for beach bums and thrill-seekers of the sea. Not to forget the Pedra de Lume salt flats, an otherworldly spectacle on this otherwise flat, desert-like terrain.

Boa Vista, aptly named "Good View," doesn't skimp on scenic wonders. Its coastlines are a feast for the eyes, and its beaches a sanctuary for nesting sea turtles, especially the protected shores of Ervatão. And if you're lucky, you might catch a glimpse of whales playing in the distance.

Fogo stands proud with Pico do Fogo, its fiery heart, an active volcano that last showed its might in 2014. This island's rich volcanic soil nurtures vineyards and coffee beans, offering a rugged backdrop for those who dare to hike its slopes.

São Vicente pulses with a beat all its own, especially in Mindelo, the cultural heartbeat of Cape Verde. It's a place where music fills the air, and the nightlife dances till dawn.

São Nicolau, with its rugged mountains and serene beaches, offers a slice of untouched Cape Verdean life, away from the tourist trails.

Maio whispers the promise of peace, with its endless beaches and a vibe that slows time itself, inviting you to breathe, relax, and simply be.

Brava, the smallest of the inhabited islands, is a green oasis of tranquility, dotted with villages where flowers outnumber people, a hidden gem for those seeking solace in nature's embrace.

And then there's **Santa Luzia**, untouched by human habitation, calling out to the wild at heart for exploration.

Cape Verde, with its mosaic of islands, each with its distinct allure, binds a common thread of warm welcomes and rich, vibrant culture. Whether it's adventure, relaxation, or a deep cultural plunge you seek, these islands beckon with open arms.

A Glimpse into Cape Verde's History

The history of Cape Verde is a mesmerizing blend, spun from the threads of African, Portuguese, and Brazilian influences. These islands, once untouched, came to life with the arrival of Portuguese explorers in the 15th century. Positioned on the pulsing veins of the Atlantic slave trade, Cape Verde soon became a crucial waypoint for vessels navigating the complex web of commerce tying Africa to Europe and the Americas.

This confluence of cultures breathes through the islands' melodies, flavors, and traditions. Kriolu, the Creole tongue, stands as a testament to this blend, weaving Portuguese and African dialects into a single fabric of communication.

The journey through the 19th and 20th centuries was marked by trials - droughts and economic strains nudged many to seek new horizons, especially in the United States, where they sowed the seeds of vibrant expatriate communities.

1975 was a watershed year when Cape Verde unfurled its flag of independence from Portugal, embarking on a journey as the Republic of Cape Verde. The years that followed saw the nation carve a path of progress and democratic governance, a beacon of stability in a region often shadowed by turmoil.

In today's Cape Verde, the rich tapestry of its heritage and history is celebrated with pride. A strong national identity, rooted in both African and Portuguese heritage, pulsates through the islands. While the past is revered and remembered, it's the resilient, forward-looking spirit of the Cape Verdean people that shapes the narrative of today and tomorrow.

Understanding the Climate and Geography

Cape Verde, with its clutch of islands, dances across a spectrum of climates and terrains, each island wearing its unique persona shaped by the whims of weather and geography.

Perched in the subtropical belt, the archipelago basks in a temperate, mostly dry embrace throughout the year. The mercury hovers around a comfortable 25°C (77°F), offering a steady warmth with scant variation as seasons glide by. Yet, the islands flirt with microclimates, their diverse topographies scripting local weather tales.

The islands split into two main ensembles: the Barlavento (windward) islands to the north, including gems like Santo Antão, São Vicente, and the sandy realms of Sal and Boa Vista; and the Sotavento (leeward) islands to the south, with Maio, Santiago, and the volcanic Fogo among them.

Barlavento plays host to flatter, arid landscapes where sandy beaches stretch under a ceaseless sun, making them havens for beach lovers and water sports aficionados, all thanks to the sunny disposition and the kiss of constant winds.

Sotavento, in contrast, wears its landscapes with a bit more flourish — mountainous terrains drape these islands, nurturing lush greenery and a patchwork of agriculture. Santiago flaunts a mosaic from dry plains to verdant valleys, while Fogo boasts its volcanic pride and Brava blooms as the "island of flowers" with its floral bounty.

Rain whispers its presence fleetingly between August and October, the "tempo das chuvas" or rainy season, though its touch varies widely across the islands and from year to year.

The surrounding seas play their part too, with the cool Canary Current ensuring the climate stays agreeable. The trade winds, especially the Harmattan from the Sahara, occasionally sweep in with dust and a cooler breath during winter.

Cape Verde's climate and geography unfurl a tapestry of experiences — from sun-soaked beach lounging to treks across rugged, volcanic vistas. Whether your heart seeks the gentle caress of the sun or the thrill of mountain trails, there's an island calling your name.

16|Cape Verde Travel Guide

Discovering Cape Verde

Top 25 Must-Visit Attractions

Cape Verde is a diverse and captivating archipelago off the west coast of Africa, offering a range of attractions for travelers of all tastes and budgets. Whether you are looking for sun, sea, sand, culture, adventure, or nature, you will find something to suit your preferences in this island nation. Here are some of the best places to visit in Cape Verde in 2024:

Praia de Santa Maria: This is the main tourist hub of Sal, where you will find a variety of hotels, restaurants, bars, shops, and entertainment options. Santa Maria has a long and beautiful beach that stretches for 8 kilometers, offering plenty of space for sunbathing and water sports. You can also enjoy the colorful and vibrant atmosphere of the town, with its cobbled streets, colonial buildings, and local markets.

Pedra de Lume Salt Crater: This is a natural wonder of Sal, where you can see the remains of a salt mine that was once the main source of income for the island. The salt pans are located in the crater of an extinct volcano, creating a surreal and scenic landscape. You can also experience the sensation of floating in the salty water, which is said to have therapeutic benefits for the skin and health.

Santa Monica Beach: This is one of the most beautiful beaches in Cape Verde, located on the island of Boa Vista. It is a secluded and pristine stretch of white sand and turquoise water, surrounded by dunes and cliffs. It is a perfect spot for relaxing, swimming, and enjoying the views. You might even spot some turtles or whales in the sea.

Praia de Chaves: This is another stunning beach on Boa Vista, where you can enjoy the sun, the sand, and the surf. It is a popular spot for kite surfing, as the wind and waves are ideal for this sport. You can also explore the nearby village of Rabil, where you can see the traditional pottery and handicrafts of the locals.

Viveiro, Botanical Garden & Zoo di Terra: This is a unique attraction on Sal, where you can see a variety of plants and animals in a natural setting. It is a project that aims to preserve and promote the biodiversity of Cape Verde, as well as educate and entertain visitors. You can stroll through the paths, pet the animals, have a picnic on the grass, or meditate in the walking-meditation labyrinth. You can also enjoy a drink or a snack at the bar, or buy some souvenirs at the shop.

Projeto Biodiversidade: This is a conservation project on Sal, where you can learn about the endangered loggerhead sea turtles that nest on the island. You can visit the turtle hatchery on the beach, where you can see the eggs and the baby turtles, and learn about the work done to protect them. You can also join a night tour to see the adult turtles laying their eggs on the sand, or a morning tour to see the hatchlings making their way to the sea.

Cidade Velha: This is the oldest colonial city in Cape Verde, and a UNESCO World Heritage Site. It is located on the island of Santiago, and it was the first European settlement in the tropics. It was once a prosperous port and a center of the slave trade, but it was also attacked by pirates and rival powers. You can see the historical and cultural monuments of the city, such as the fort, the cathedral, the royal palace, and the slave market. You can also enjoy the views of the coast and the mountains from the city.

Fogo Island: This is the most volcanic island in Cape Verde, and home to the highest peak in the country, Pico do Fogo. It is an active volcano that last erupted in 2014, creating a dramatic and diverse landscape of lava fields, craters, and slopes. You can hike up the volcano, or explore the surrounding villages, where you can see the traditional architecture, agriculture, and culture of the islanders. You can also taste the local wine and coffee, which are produced from the fertile volcanic soil.

Mindelo: This is the cultural capital of Cape Verde, and the second largest city in the country. It is located on the island of Sao Vicente, and it is known for its lively and artistic atmosphere. It is the birthplace of the national music of Cape Verde, called morna, which is a blend of Portuguese, African, and Brazilian influences. You can listen to live music at the bars and clubs or visit the cultural center, where you can see exhibitions and performances. You can also see the colonial and colorful buildings of the city, or take a ferry to the nearby island of Santo Antao, which is famous for its natural beauty and hiking trails.

Boa Vista Island: This is the third largest and the most eastern island in Cape Verde, and it is known for its desert-like landscape and its stunning beaches. It is a paradise for nature lovers and adventure seekers, as you can see a variety of wildlife, such as birds, turtles, whales, and sharks. You can also enjoy activities such as quad biking, dune buggy, sailing, fishing, and diving. You can also visit the Viana desert, which is a small patch of sand dunes that were blown from the Sahara.

Tarrafal: This is a small town on the northern coast of Santiago, and it is a popular destination for beach lovers and history buffs. It has a beautiful bay with a golden sand beach and clear blue water, where you can relax, swim, or snorkel. You can also visit the Tarrafal camp, which was a prison for political opponents of the Portuguese colonial regime. You can see the cells, the torture chambers, and the cemetery, and learn about the history and the stories of the prisoners.

Pedra de Lume: This is another natural attraction of Sal, where you can witness the amazing phenomenon of the "Blue Eye". It is a natural pool that is formed by a hole in the rocks, where the sunlight reflects on the water and creates a blue eye effect. It is a beautiful and mysterious sight, and you can also swim in the pool, which is connected to the sea by an underwater tunnel.

Sao Filipe: This is the largest and the most important town on Fogo island, and it is a charming and colorful place to visit. It has a colonial and historical architecture, with whitewashed houses and red roofs. It also has a lively and festive atmosphere, especially during the annual Bandeira festival, which is a celebration of the local culture and traditions. You can see the parades, the dances, the music, and the costumes, and join the fun.
Praia: This is the capital and the largest city of Cape Verde, and it is located on the island of Santiago. It is a modern and cosmopolitan city, with a mix of African and European

influences. It has a variety of attractions, such as museums, markets, monuments, and parks. You can also see the contrast between the old and the new parts of the city, such as the Plateau, which is the historical and cultural center, and the Palmarejo, which is the commercial and residential area.

Ribeira Grande: This is a picturesque town on the island of Santo Antao, and it is situated in a valley surrounded by green mountains and rivers. It is a peaceful and scenic place, where you can enjoy the nature and the culture of the island. You can see the traditional houses, the churches, the bridges, and the water mills, or visit the local markets, where you can buy fresh fruits, vegetables, and handicrafts. You can also hike along the trails, or take a bus or a taxi to explore other parts of the island.

Sal Rei: This is the main town on Boa Vista Island, and it is a quiet and relaxing place to stay. It has a laid-back and friendly atmosphere, with a few hotels, restaurants, bars, and shops. It also has a nice beach, where you can swim, sunbathe, or watch the fishing boats. You can also visit the nearby islet of Sal Rei, where you can see the ruins of a fort that was built by the Portuguese to defend the island from pirates.

Maio Island: This is one of the least visited and most unspoiled islands in Cape Verde, and it is a perfect destination for those who want to escape the crowds and enjoy nature. It has a flat and dry landscape, with sandy beaches, salt flats, and acacia forests. It is also home to a variety of birds, such as flamingos, herons, and pelicans. You can relax on the beach, or visit the small towns and villages, where you can see the local life and culture

Sao Pedro Beach: Nestled on Sao Vicente, close to the airport, this expansive beach marries fine sands with azure waters. It's a windsurfer's dream, with conditions that promise an exhilarating ride. Bars and restaurants line the shore, offering refreshments and a unique view of planes soaring into the sky.

Ribeira do Paul: Santo Antao presents this breathtaking valley, cradled by a river and bursting with life. Here, agriculture thrives—bananas, sugar cane, coffee, and mangoes flourish under the watchful care of traditional irrigation methods. Whether by foot or by local transport, exploring this verdant paradise reveals the island's heart and soul.

Praia de Fontona: On the island of Brava, this secluded beach is a hidden treasure. It's a snorkeler's paradise, where the waters unveil a vibrant underwater ballet of fish and coral. The beach's tranquility is perfect for those seeking peace, with the village of Fontona nearby to explore local culture.

Monte Gordo Natural Park: Sao Nicolau's pride, this mountain range spans the island's heart, a sanctuary for endemic wildlife and breathtaking vistas. The climb to Monte Gordo, the island's zenith, rewards adventurers with panoramic views that stretch to infinity.

Praia de Morabeza: Over on Maio, this beach is a stretch of paradise. White sands and turquoise waters are framed by palm trees, inviting relaxation and immersion in nature's beauty. Keep an eye out for turtles or dolphins, who might grace you with their presence.

Praia de Tarrafal: On Santiago, this bay offers a golden beach hugged by clear blue waters, ideal for unwinding or exploring underwater marvels. The nearby Tarrafal camp, a somber reminder of history, offers a deep dive into the stories of resilience and struggle.

Pristine Beaches of Cape Verde

Cape Verde is a diverse and captivating archipelago off the west coast of Africa, offering a range of attractions for travelers of all tastes and budgets. Whether you are looking for sun, sea, sand, culture, adventure, or nature, you will find something to suit your preferences in this island nation. One of the main draws of Cape Verde is its pristine beaches, which are among the best in the world. With its year-round pleasant climate, Cape Verde is the perfect destination for those seeking sun, relaxation, and an escape from the hustle and bustle of everyday life.

In this subchapter, we will explore some of the top beaches that Cape Verde has to offer, as well as provide some useful information on how to get there, what to do, and where to stay. Whether you prefer the tranquility of secluded spots or the lively atmosphere of popular tourist destinations, Cape Verde has something for everyone. So, grab your sunscreen, put on your flip-flops, and let's embark on a virtual journey to discover the pristine beaches of Cape Verde.

Praia de Santa Maria

This is the main tourist hub of Sal, where you will find a variety of hotels, restaurants, bars, shops, and entertainment options. Santa Maria has a long and beautiful beach that stretches for 8 kilometres, offering plenty of space for sunbathing and water sports. You can also enjoy the colorful and vibrant atmosphere of the town, with its cobbled streets, colonial buildings, and local markets.

How to get there

The easiest way to get to Praia de Santa Maria is to fly to Sal International Airport, which is located in the capital, Espargos. The airport receives flights from several European and African cities, as well as from other Cape Verdean islands. From the airport, you can take a taxi or a bus to Santa Maria, which is about 18 kilometres away. The taxi fare is around 10 euros, and the bus fare is around 1 euro. Alternatively, you can rent a car or a scooter at the airport or in the town.

What to do

There are plenty of things to do in and around Praia de Santa Maria, depending on your interests and preferences. Some of the most popular activities are:

Swimming and Snorkeling: The water in Santa Maria is calm and clear, making it ideal for swimming and snorkeling. You can see a variety of fish and coral, as well as turtles and dolphins if you are lucky. You can rent snorkeling equipment at the beach, or join a guided tour to explore the best spots.

Kite surfing and windsurfing: Santa Maria is one of the best places in the world for kite surfing and windsurfing, as the wind and waves are perfect for these sports. You can rent equipment at the beach, or take lessons at one of the many schools and clubs. You can also join competitions and events, or watch the professionals perform amazing tricks and stunts.

Whale watching and turtle watching: Santa Maria is a great place to see some of the amazing marine wildlife that Cape Verde has to offer. You can join a boat tour to see the humpback whales that visit the island between March and May, or the sperm whales that can be seen all year round. You can also join a night tour to see the loggerhead turtles that nest on the beach between June and October, or a morning tour to see the hatchlings making their way to the sea.

Fishing and sailing: Santa Maria is a fishing town, and you can experience the local culture and tradition by joining a fishing trip or a sailing trip. You can catch a variety of fish, such as tuna, marlin, swordfish, and shark, or just enjoy the views and the breeze. You can also rent a boat or a yacht, or join a cruise, to explore the coast and the nearby islands.

Where to stay
There are many accommodation options in and around Praia de Santa Maria, ranging from budget to luxury. Some of the best places to stay are:

Hotel Morabeza: This is a four-star hotel that is located on the beach, offering stunning views and easy access to the water. It has spacious and comfortable rooms, with balconies, air conditioning, and free Wi-Fi. It also has a restaurant, a bar, a pool, a gym, and a spa. The hotel organizes various activities and excursions, such as fishing, sailing, diving, and golf. The price per night is around 100 euros.

Oasis Salinas Sea: This is a five-star hotel that is located on the beach, offering luxury and comfort. It has modern and elegant rooms, with balconies, air conditioning, and free Wi-Fi. It also has a restaurant, a bar, a pool, a gym, and a spa. The hotel organizes various activities and excursions, such as kite surfing, windsurfing, snorkeling, and whale watching. The price per night is around 150 euros.

Hotel da Luz: This is a three-star hotel that is located near the beach, offering convenience and value. It has cozy and clean rooms, with air conditioning and free Wi-Fi. It also has a restaurant, a bar, and a pool. The hotel organizes various activities and excursions, such as fishing, sailing, diving, and turtle watching. The price per night is around 50 euros.

Praia de Estoril

This is a beach on the island of Boa Vista, and it is located near the town of Sal Rei. It is a long and wide beach, with soft sand and calm water. It is a good place for swimming, snorkeling, or relaxing on the sun loungers. You can also find some bars and restaurants along the beach, where you can have a drink or a meal, and enjoy the views and the breeze.

How to get there
The easiest way to get to Praia de Estoril is to fly to Boa Vista International Airport, which is located in the capital, Rabil. The airport receives flights from several European and African cities, as well as from other Cape Verdean islands. From the airport, you can take a taxi or a bus to Sal Rei, which is about 6 kilometers away. The taxi fare is around 5 euros, and the bus fare is around 0.5 euros. Alternatively, you can rent a car or a scooter at the airport or in the town.

What to do
There are plenty of things to do in and around Praia de Estoril, depending on your interests and preferences. Some of the most popular activities are:

Swimming and Snorkelling: The water in Praia de Estoril is clear and warm, making it ideal for swimming and snorkelling. You can see a variety of fish and coral, as well as turtles and dolphins if you are lucky. You can rent snorkelling equipment at the beach, or join a guided tour to explore the best spots.

Quad biking and dune buggy: Praia de Estoril is surrounded by dunes and desert, offering a unique and adventurous landscape to explore. You can rent a quad bike or a dune buggy at the beach, or join a guided tour to discover the hidden gems and the stunning views of the island. You can also visit the Viana desert, which is a small patch of sand dunes that were blown from the Sahara1.

Sailing and fishing: Praia de Estoril is a great place to enjoy the sea and the wind, as you can sail along the coast and the nearby islands. You can rent a boat or a yacht, or join a cruise, to experience the beauty and the tranquility of the ocean. You can also try your luck at fishing, as the waters are rich with tuna, marlin, swordfish, and shark.

Where to stay
There are many accommodation options in and around Praia de Estoril, ranging from budget to luxury. Some of the best places to stay are:

Hotel Estoril e Residence Cardeal: This is a three-star hotel that is located on the beach, offering convenience and comfort. It has simple and clean rooms, with balconies, air conditioning, and free Wi-Fi. It also has a restaurant, a bar, and a pool. The hotel organizes various activities and excursions, such as quad biking, sailing, diving, and turtle watching. The price per night is around 40 euros.

Hotel Riu Karamboa: This is a five-star hotel that is located on the beach, offering luxury and elegance. It has spacious and stylish rooms, with balconies, air conditioning, and free Wi-Fi. It also has a restaurant, a bar, a pool, a gym, and a spa. The hotel organizes various activities and excursions, such as kite surfing, windsurfing, snorkeling, and whale watching. The price per night is around 200 euros.

Casa Boteto: This is a guesthouse that is located near the beach, offering value and charm. It has cozy and colorful rooms, with air conditioning and free Wi-Fi. It also has a shared kitchen, a lounge, and a terrace. The guesthouse organizes various activities and excursions, such as fishing, sailing, diving, and turtle watching. The price per night is around 30 euros.

Praia de Tarrafal

This is a beach on the island of Santiago, and it is located near the town of Tarrafal. It is a beautiful bay with a golden sand beach and a clear blue water, where you can relax, swim, or snorkel. You can also visit the Tarrafal camp, which was a prison for political opponents of the Portuguese colonial regime. You can see the cells, the torture chambers, and the cemetery, and learn about the history and the stories of the prisoners.

How to get there

The easiest way to get to Praia de Tarrafal is to fly to Praia International Airport, which is located in the capital, Praia. The airport receives flights from several European and African cities, as well as from other Cape Verdean islands. From the airport, you can take a taxi or a bus to Tarrafal, which is about 70 kilometres away. The taxi fare is around 40 euros, and the bus fare is around 4 euros. Alternatively, you can rent a car or a scooter at the airport or in the city.

What to do

There are plenty of things to do in and around Praia de Tarrafal, depending on your interests and preferences. Some of the most popular activities are:

Swimming and Snorkelling: The water in Praia de Tarrafal is calm and clear, making it ideal for swimming and snorkelling. You can see a variety of fish and coral, as well as turtles and dolphins if you are lucky. You can rent snorkelling equipment at the beach, or join a guided tour to explore the best spots.

Hiking and Biking: Praia de Tarrafal is surrounded by green mountains and valleys, offering a scenic and adventurous landscape to explore. You can hike or bike along the trails, or join a guided tour to discover the hidden gems and the stunning views of the island. You can also visit the nearby town of Ribeira Grande, where you can see the traditional architecture, culture, and handicrafts of the locals.

Visiting the Tarrafal camp: Praia de Tarrafal is also known for its historical and cultural significance, as it was the site of a prison camp that was used by the Portuguese colonial regime to detain and torture political opponents. You can visit the camp, which is now a museum, and see the cells, the torture chambers, and the cemetery, where many prisoners died. You can also learn about the history and the stories of the prisoners, and pay tribute to their memory and struggle.

Where to stay
There are many accommodation options in and around Praia de Tarrafal, ranging from budget to luxury. Some of the best places to stay are:

Hotel Tarrafal: This is a three-star hotel that is located on the beach, offering convenience and comfort. It has simple and clean rooms, with balconies, air conditioning, and free Wi-Fi. It also has a restaurant, a bar, and a pool. The hotel organizes various activities and excursions, such as hiking, biking, diving, and fishing. The price per night is around 50 euros.

King Fisher Resort: This is a four-star hotel that is located on the beach, offering luxury and elegance. It has spacious and stylish rooms, with balconies, air conditioning, and free Wi-Fi. It also has a restaurant, a bar, a pool, a gym, and a spa. The hotel organizes various activities and excursions, such as kite surfing, windsurfing, snorkeling, and whale watching. The price per night is around 100 euros.

Baia Verde: This is a guesthouse that is located near the beach, offering value and charm. It has cozy and colorful rooms, with air conditioning and free Wi-Fi. It also has a shared kitchen, a lounge, and a terrace. The guesthouse organizes various activities and excursions, such as fishing, sailing, diving, and turtle watching. The price per night is around 30 euros.

Praia de Buracona

This is a beach on the island of Sal, and it is located near the town of Palmeira. It is a small and rocky beach, with clear water and colorful fish. It is a perfect spot for snorkelling, as you can see the coral reef and the marine life. You can also witness the amazing phenomenon of the "Blue Eye", which is a natural pool that is formed by a hole in the rocks, where the sunlight reflects on the water and creates a blue eye effect.

How to get there
The easiest way to get to Praia de Buracona is to fly to Sal International Airport, which is located in the capital, Espargos. The airport receives flights from several European and African cities, as well as from other Cape Verdean islands. From the airport, you can take a taxi or a bus to Palmeira, which is about 25 kilometers away. The taxi fare is around 15 euros, and the bus fare is around 2 euros. Alternatively, you can rent a car or a scooter at the airport or in the town.

What to do
There are plenty of things to do in and around Praia de Buracona, depending on your interests and preferences. Some of the most popular activities are:

Snorkelling and diving: The water in Praia de Buracona is clear and warm, making it ideal for snorkelling and diving. You can see a variety of fish and coral, as well as turtles and dolphins if you are lucky. You can rent snorkeling or diving equipment at the beach, or join a guided tour to explore the best spots.

Visiting the Blue Eye: Praia de Buracona is also known for its natural attraction, the Blue Eye, which is a natural pool that is formed by a hole in the rocks, where the sunlight reflects on the water and creates a blue eye effect. It is a beautiful and mysterious sight, and you can also swim in the pool, which is connected to the sea by an underwater tunnel. The best time to see the Blue Eye is between 11 am and 1 pm, when the sun is at the right angle.

Relaxing and sunbathing: Praia de Buracona is a small and quiet beach, where you can relax and enjoy the nature. You can sunbathe on the rocks, or find a shady spot under the palm trees. You can also have a picnic on the beach, or visit the nearby café, where you can have a drink or a snack, and use the facilities.

Where to stay
There are not many accommodation options in and around Praia de Buracona, as it is a remote and undeveloped area. However, you can find some places to stay nearby, such as:

Hotel da Luz: This is a three-star hotel that is located near the beach of Palmeira, offering convenience and value. It has cozy and clean rooms, with air conditioning and free Wi-Fi. It also has a restaurant, a bar, and a pool. The hotel organizes various activities and excursions, such as fishing, sailing, diving, and turtle watching. The price per night is around 50 euros.

Murdeira Village Resort: This is a four-star hotel that is located near the beach of Murdeira, offering luxury and comfort. It has spacious and elegant rooms, with balconies, air conditioning, and free Wi-Fi. It also has a restaurant, a bar, a pool, a gym, and a spa. The hotel organizes various activities and excursions, such as kite surfing, windsurfing, snorkelling, and whale watching. The price per night is around 100 euros.

Camping: This is a budget option that is available near the beach of Buracona, offering adventure and nature. You can pitch your tent on the rocks, or rent a tent at the café. You can also use the facilities of the café, such as the toilets, the showers, and the electricity. The price per night is around 10 euros.

Hiking Trails and Natural Wonders

Cape Verde is not only a paradise for beach lovers, but also for hikers and nature enthusiasts. The islands offer a variety of trails and natural wonders, ranging from volcanic peaks and craters, to lush valleys and waterfalls, to desert dunes and oases. You can experience the diversity and beauty of Cape Verde's landscapes, as well as the culture and history of its people, by exploring them on foot. Whether you are looking for a challenging adventure or a relaxing stroll, Cape Verde has something for everyone.

In this subchapter, we will explore some of the top hiking trails and natural wonders that Cape Verde has to offer, as well as provide some useful information on how to get there, what to do, and where to stay. Whether you prefer the rugged and dramatic scenery of Fogo and Santo Antao, or the serene and tranquil scenery of Maio and Sao Nicolau, Cape Verde will surprise and delight you with its natural treasures. So, grab your hiking boots, put on your hat, and let's embark on a virtual journey to discover the hiking trails and natural wonders of Cape Verde.

Pico do Fogo

This is the highest peak in Cape Verde, and it is located on the island of Fogo. It is an active volcano that last erupted in 2014, creating a dramatic and diverse landscape of lava fields, craters, and slopes. You can hike up the volcano, or join a guided tour, and see the amazing views of the island and the sea. You can also explore the surrounding villages, where you can see the traditional architecture, agriculture, and culture of the islanders. You can also taste the local wine and coffee, which are produced from the fertile volcanic soil.

How to get there
The easiest way to get to Pico do Fogo is to fly to Fogo International Airport, which is located in the capital, Sao Filipe. The airport receives flights from several Cape Verdean islands, as well as from Praia, the capital of the country. From the airport, you can take a taxi or a bus to the town of Cha das Caldeiras, which is the starting point of the hike. The taxi fare is around 20 euros, and the bus fare is around 2 euros. Alternatively, you can rent a car or a scooter at the airport or in the town.

What to do
There are plenty of things to do in and around Pico do Fogo, depending on your interests and preferences. Some of the most popular activities are:

Hiking and climbing: The main attraction of Pico do Fogo is the hike to the summit, which is a challenging and rewarding experience. The hike takes about 6 hours round trip, and it requires good fitness, sturdy shoes, and alpine experience. You can hike on your own, or join a guided tour, which can provide you with equipment, transportation, and information. You can also climb the crater rim, which is a more difficult and dangerous option, but it offers a closer view of the lava lake and the steam vents.

Exploring and learning: Pico do Fogo is not only a natural wonder, but also a cultural and historical one. You can explore the surrounding villages, such as Portela and Bangaeira, which were partially destroyed by the 2014 eruption, and see how the locals have rebuilt their lives and homes. You can also learn about the history and the stories of the volcano, and the impact it has had on the island and its people. You can visit the museum, the church, and the school, or talk to the guides and the residents.

Tasting and shopping: Pico do Fogo is also a place of gastronomy and handicrafts, as the volcanic soil and the climate produce some of the best wine and coffee in Cape Verde. You can taste the local products, such as the Fogo wine, which is made from the endemic grape variety called Manecon, or the Fogo coffee, which is grown at high altitudes and roasted by hand. You can also buy some souvenirs, such as pottery, paintings, and jewelry, which are made by the local artisans.

Where to stay

There are not many accommodation options in and around Pico do Fogo, as it is a remote and undeveloped area. However, you can find some places to stay nearby, such as:

Casa Marisa: This is a guesthouse that is located in Cha das Caldeiras, offering convenience and comfort. It has simple and clean rooms, with private bathrooms, hot water, and free Wi-Fi. It also has a restaurant, a bar, and a terrace. The guesthouse organizes various activities and excursions, such as hiking, climbing, and wine tasting. The price per night is around 40 euros.

Hotel Xaguate: This is a four-star hotel that is located in Sao Filipe, offering luxury and elegance. It has spacious and stylish rooms, with balconies, air conditioning, and free Wi-Fi. It also has a restaurant, a bar, a pool, a gym, and a spa. The hotel organizes various activities and excursions, such as hiking, climbing, and wine tasting. The price per night is around 80 euros.

Camping: This is a budget option that is available near the summit of Pico do Fogo, offering adventure and nature. You can pitch your tent on the lava field, or rent a tent at the crater rim. You can also use the facilities of the guides, such as the toilets, the showers, and the kitchen. The price per night is around 10 euros.

Cova do Paul

This is a natural attraction on the island of Santo Antao, and it is a huge crater that was formed by a volcanic eruption. It is now filled with fertile soil and lush vegetation, creating a green oasis in the middle of the island. You can hike down to the crater, or take a bus or a taxi, and see the farms, the crops, and the flowers that grow there. You can also visit the nearby town of Paul, where you can see the local life and culture.

How to get there
The easiest way to get to Cova do Paul is to fly to Sao Vicente International Airport, which is located in the capital, Mindelo. The airport receives flights from several Cape Verdean islands, as well as from Praia, the capital of the country. From the airport, you can take a ferry or a boat to the island of Santo Antao, which takes about an hour. From the port of Porto Novo, you can take a taxi or a bus to the town of Ribeira Grande, which is about 20 kilometers away. From there, you can take another taxi or bus to Cova do Paul, which is about 10 kilometers away.

What to do

There are plenty of things to do in and around Cova do Paul, depending on your interests and preferences. Some of the most popular activities are:

Hiking and biking: The main attraction of Cova do Paul is the hike to the crater, which is a scenic and rewarding experience. The hike takes about 3 hours round trip, and it requires good fitness, sturdy shoes, and water. You can hike on your own, or join a guided tour, which can provide you with equipment, transportation, and information. You can also bike along the trails, or join a guided tour, which can provide you with bikes, helmets, and maps.

Exploring and learning: Cova do Paul is not only a natural wonder, but also a cultural and historical one. You can explore the surrounding villages, such as Cabo de Ribeira, Pico da Cruz, and Janela, which are part of the Biosphere Reserve of Santo Antao. You can see the traditional architecture, agriculture, and handicrafts of the locals, as well as the endemic plants and animals of the island. You can also learn about the history and the stories of the crater, and the impact it has had on the island and its people.

Tasting and shopping: Cova do Paul is also a place of gastronomy and handicrafts, as the fertile soil and the climate produce some of the best fruits, vegetables, and flowers in Cape Verde. You can taste the local products, such as the bananas, the mangoes, the papayas, and the roses, or buy some souvenirs, such as jams, honey, and baskets, which are made by the local artisans.

Where to stay

There are not many accommodation options in and around Cova do Paul, as it is a remote and undeveloped area. However, you can find some places to stay nearby, such as:

Casa Cavoquinho: This is a guesthouse that is located in the village of Cabo de Ribeira, offering convenience and comfort. It has simple and clean rooms, with private bathrooms, hot water, and free Wi-Fi. It also has a restaurant, a bar, and a terrace. The guesthouse organizes various activities and excursions, such as hiking, biking, and wine tasting. The price per night is around 40 euros.

Pedracin Village: This is a four-star hotel that is located in the village of Pico da Cruz, offering luxury and elegance. It has spacious and stylish rooms, with balconies, air conditioning, and free Wi-Fi. It also has a restaurant, a bar, a pool, a gym, and a spa. The hotel organizes various activities and excursions, such as hiking, biking, and wine tasting. The price per night is around 80 euros.

Camping: This is a budget option that is available near the crater of Cova do Paul, offering adventure and nature. You can pitch your tent on the grass, or rent a tent at the crater rim. You can also use the facilities of the guides, such as the toilets, the showers, and the kitchen. The price per night is around 10 euros.

Praia de Fontona

This is a beach on the island of Brava, and it is one of the most beautiful and secluded beaches in Cape Verde. It is a small and rocky beach, with clear water and colorful fish. It is a perfect spot for snorkelling, as you can see the coral reef and the marine life.

You can also relax on the beach, or visit the nearby village of Fontona, where you can see the local life and culture.

How to get there
The easiest way to get to Praia de Fontona is to fly to Fogo International Airport, which is located in the capital, Sao Filipe. The airport receives flights from several Cape Verdean islands, as well as from Praia, the capital of the country. From the airport, you can take a ferry or a boat to the island of Brava, which takes about an hour. From the port of Furna, you can take a taxi or a bus to the village of Fontona, which is about 5 kilometres away.

What to do
There are plenty of things to do in and around Praia de Fontona, depending on your interests and preferences. Some of the most popular activities are:

Snorkelling and diving: The water in Praia de Fontona is clear and warm, making it ideal for snorkeling and diving. You can see a variety of fish and coral, as well as turtles and dolphins if you are lucky. You can rent snorkelling or diving equipment at the beach, or join a guided tour to explore the best spots.

Hiking and biking: Praia de Fontona is surrounded by green mountains and valleys, offering a scenic and adventurous landscape to explore. You can hike or bike along the trails, or join a guided tour to discover the hidden gems and the stunning views of the island. You can also visit the nearby town of Nova Sintra, where you can see the traditional architecture, culture, and handicrafts of the locals.

Relaxing and sunbathing: Praia de Fontona is a small and quiet beach, where you can relax and enjoy the nature. You can sunbathe on the rocks, or find a shady spot under the palm trees. You can also have a picnic on the beach, or visit the nearby café, where you can have a drink or a snack, and use the facilities.

Where to stay

There are not many accommodation options in and around Praia de Fontona, as it is a remote and undeveloped area. However, you can find some places to stay nearby, such as:

Hotel Cruz Grande: This is a three-star hotel that is located in the town of Nova Sintra, offering convenience and comfort. It has simple and clean rooms, with private bathrooms, hot water, and free Wi-Fi. It also has a restaurant, a bar, and a terrace. The hotel organizes various activities and excursions, such as hiking, biking, and snorkeling. The price per night is around 40 euros.

Pousada da Brava: This is a four-star hotel that is located in the town of Nova Sintra, offering luxury and elegance. It has spacious and stylish rooms, with balconies, air conditioning, and free Wi-Fi. It also has a restaurant, a bar, a pool, a gym, and a spa. The hotel organizes various activities and excursions, such as hiking, biking, and snorkelling. The price per night is around 80 euros.

Camping: This is a budget option that is available near the beach of Praia de Fontona, offering adventure and nature. You can pitch your tent on the rocks, or rent a tent at the café. You can also use the facilities of the café, such as the toilets, the showers, and the electricity. The price per night is around 10 euros.

Praia de Morabeza

This is a beach on the island of Maio, and it is located near the town of Vila do Maio. It is a long and wide beach, with white sand and turquoise water, surrounded by palm trees and dunes. It is a peaceful and relaxing place, where you can swim, sunbathe, or enjoy the nature. You might even spot some turtles or dolphins in the sea.

How to get there

The easiest way to get to Praia de Morabeza is to fly to Maio International Airport, which is located in the capital, Vila do Maio. The airport receives flights from several Cape Verdean islands, as well as from Praia, the capital of the country. From the airport, you can take a taxi or a bus to the beach, which is about 2 kilometers away. The taxi fare is around 2 euros, and the bus fare is around 0.2 euros. Alternatively, you can rent a car or a scooter at the airport or in the town.

What to do

There are plenty of things to do in and around Praia de Morabeza, depending on your interests and preferences. Some of the most popular activities are:

Swimming and snorkelling: The water in Praia de Morabeza is calm and clear, making it ideal for swimming and snorkelling. You can see a variety of fish and coral, as well as turtles and dolphins if you are lucky.

Snorkelling and diving: The water in Praia de Morabeza is calm and clear, making it ideal for snorkelling and diving. You can see a variety of fish and coral, as well as turtles and dolphins if you are lucky. You can rent snorkelling or diving equipment at the beach, or join a guided tour to explore the best spots.

Relaxing and sunbathing: Praia de Morabeza is a small and quiet beach, where you can relax and enjoy the nature. You can sunbathe on the sand, or find a shady spot under the palm trees. You can also have a picnic on the beach, or visit the nearby café, where you can have a drink or a snack, and use the facilities.

Where to stay
There are not many accommodation options in and around Praia de Morabeza, as it is a remote and undeveloped area. However, you can find some places to stay nearby, such as:

Hotel Marilu: This is a three-star hotel that is located in the town of Vila do Maio, offering convenience and comfort. It has simple and clean rooms, with private bathrooms, hot water, and free Wi-Fi. It also has a restaurant, a bar, and a terrace. The hotel organizes various activities and excursions, such as hiking, biking, and snorkelling. The price per night is around 40 euros.

Stella Maris Village: This is a four-star hotel that is located in the town of Vila do Maio, offering luxury and elegance. It has spacious and stylish rooms, with balconies, air conditioning, and free Wi-Fi. It also has a restaurant, a bar, a pool, a gym, and a spa. The hotel organizes various activities and excursions, such as kite surfing, windsurfing, snorkelling, and whale watching. The price per night is around 80 euros.

Camping: This is a budget option that is available near the beach of Praia de Morabeza, offering adventure and nature. You can pitch your tent on the sand, or rent a tent at the café. You can also use the facilities of the café, such as the toilets, the showers, and the electricity. The price per night is around 10 euros.

Culinary Delights: A Taste of Cape Verde

Cape Verde's culinary scene is a testament to its rich cultural tapestry, blending local traditions with a dash of international flair. Among the islands, certain spots stand out for their delectable offerings, providing both a feast for the senses and a glimpse into the heart of Cape Verdean gastronomy.

Tortuga: Nestled near Sao Filipe on the island of Fogo, Tortuga is a culinary haven specializing in seafood and local delicacies. Diners can delight in dishes like cachupa, grilled tuna, and succulent lobster, all while soaking in the views from a sun-drenched terrace overlooking the sea. The ambiance is complemented by Tortuga's warm and inviting service, making it a must-visit for any food enthusiast.

Vista Mar: Perched on Santiago, near the tranquil town of Tarrafal, Vista Mar serves as both a hotel and a culinary destination. The restaurant offers a diverse menu, featuring everything from fresh fish and chicken to pasta and salads. Guests can dine on a sun terrace, enjoy the expansive sea view, or take a dip in the pool, making it a perfect spot for a leisurely meal that captures the essence of island dining.

L' atelier - cap vert: On Santiago, close to the bustling city of Praia, L' atelier presents a fusion of Cape Verdean and French cuisine. The menu tempts with couscous, crepes, and an assortment of pastries, set against a backdrop of a cozy and colorful atmosphere. The friendly staff enhances the dining experience, making it a cozy spot for those looking to enjoy a blend of cultures on their plate.

For those eager to dive deeper into Cape Verde's culinary culture, the streets and markets offer a taste of local life through their array of street food and snacks:

Pastel: A fried pastry filled with either fish, meat, or cheese, usually accompanied by a spicy sauce. It's a favored snack or appetizer among locals and travelers alike.

Cuscuz: A steamed corn flour cake, often enriched with coconut and sugar, flavored with cinnamon, nutmeg, or vanilla. Typically enjoyed for breakfast or dessert, it offers a sweet start or end to any day.

Grogue: Cape Verde's answer to rum, distilled from sugar cane and packed with a potent kick. It's enjoyed neat, with honey or lemon, or as the base for the national cocktail, ponche, which mixes grogue with sugar, water, and lime.

Vibrant Nightlife and Entertainment

Cape Verde is a diverse and captivating archipelago off the west coast of Africa, offering a range of attractions for travelers of all tastes and budgets. Whether you are looking for sun, sea, sand, culture, adventure, or nature, you will find something to suit your preferences in this island nation. One of the main draws of Cape Verde is its vibrant nightlife and entertainment, where music, dance, and local flavors come together to create unforgettable experiences.

If there's one thing that Cape Verde is known for and the locals are passionate about, it's music. It's an integral part of Cape Verdean culture, and it reflects the rich and varied history and influences of the islands. The blend of traditional rhythms and African, European, and Caribbean sounds create a truly magical and diverse musical scene. Cape Verdeans love to celebrate life with music and dance, and you can join them in the bars, clubs, and festivals that showcase the best of Cape Verdean music.

In this subchapter, we will explore some of the top nightlife and entertainment options that Cape Verde has to offer, as well as provide some useful information on how to get there, what to do, and where to stay. Whether you prefer the lively and popular spots of Sal and Boa Vista, or the cozy and authentic spots of Santiago and Sao Vicente, Cape Verde will surprise and delight you with its nightlife and entertainment.

Sal

Sal is the most touristy and developed island in Cape Verde, and it offers a variety of nightlife and entertainment options for all tastes and budgets. You can find everything from gentle, live music to lively nightclubs, from local bars to international restaurants, from cultural events to sports activities. Sal is the perfect destination for those who want to enjoy the sun, the sea, and the fun.

How to get there
The easiest way to get to Sal is to fly to Sal International Airport, which is located in the capital, Espargos. The airport receives flights from several European and African cities, as well as from other Cape Verdean islands. From the airport, you can take a taxi or a bus to the main tourist hub of Santa Maria, which is about 18 kilometres away. The taxi fare is around 10 euros, and the bus fare is around 1 euro. Alternatively, you can rent a car or a scooter at the airport or in the town.

What to do
There are plenty of things to do in and around Sal, depending on your interests and preferences. Some of the most popular activities are:

Live music: Sal is a great place to enjoy live music, especially Cape Verdean music genres like morna, coladeira, and funana.

You can find live music in many bars and restaurants, as well as in the main square of Santa Maria, where local bands and singers perform every night. You can also join the locals in dancing and singing along, or just sit back and enjoy the atmosphere.

Nightclubs: Sal is also a great place to party, as it has some of the best nightclubs in Cape Verde. You can find nightclubs that play a mix of local and international music, as well as themed nights and special events.

Some of the best nightclubs in Sal are:
Buddy Bar: This is a cozy and friendly bar that plays live music and karaoke every night. It also has a pool table, a dart board, and a TV screen. It is located in Santa Maria, near the beach.

Disco Pirata: This is a lively and popular nightclub that plays a mix of local and international music, as well as themed nights and special events. It also has a large dance floor, a VIP area, and a bar. It is located in Santa Maria, near the pier.

Legends: This is a modern and stylish nightclub that plays a mix of local and international music, as well as themed nights and special events. It also has a large dance floor, a VIP area, and a bar. It is located in Santa Maria, near the main square.

Restaurants: Sal is also a great place to enjoy a variety of cuisines, from local to international, from seafood to vegetarian. You can find restaurants that offer a range of dishes, as well as a range of prices, from budget to luxury. Some of the best restaurants in Sal are:

Sal Beach Club: This is a beachfront restaurant that offers a variety of dishes, such as fish, chicken, pasta, and salads. It also has a sun terrace, a sea view, and a live music. It is located in Santa Maria, on the beach.

L' atelier - cap vert: This is a restaurant that offers a fusion of Cape Verdean and French cuisine, such as couscous, crepes, and pastries. It also has a cozy and colorful atmosphere, and a friendly staff. It is located in Santa Maria, near the main square.

D-wine: This is a wine bar and restaurant that offers a variety of dishes, such as tapas, cheese, and meat. It also has a large selection of wines, as well as a live music. It is located in Santa Maria, near the pier.

Where to stay
There are many accommodation options in and around Sal, ranging from budget to luxury. Some of the best places to stay are:

Hotel Morabeza: This is a four-star hotel that is located on the beach, offering stunning views and easy access to the water. It has spacious and comfortable rooms, with balconies, air conditioning, and free Wi-Fi. It also has a restaurant, a bar, a pool, a gym, and a spa. The hotel organizes various activities and excursions, such as fishing, sailing, diving, and golf. The price per night is around 100 euros.

Oasis Salinas Sea: This is a five-star hotel that is located on the beach, offering luxury and comfort. It has modern and elegant rooms, with balconies, air conditioning, and free Wi-Fi. It also has a restaurant, a bar, a pool, a gym, and a spa. The hotel organizes various activities and excursions, such as kite surfing, windsurfing, snorkelling, and whale watching. The price per night is around 150 euros.

Hotel da Luz: This is a three-star hotel that is located near the beach, offering convenience and value. It has cozy and clean rooms, with air conditioning and free Wi-Fi. It also has a restaurant, a bar, and a pool. The hotel organizes various activities and excursions, such as fishing, sailing, diving, and turtle watching. The price per night is around 50 euros.

Boa Vista
Boa Vista is the third largest and the most eastern island in Cape Verde, and it offers a variety of nightlife and entertainment options for all tastes and budgets. You can find everything from relaxing, live music to energetic nightclubs, from local bars to international restaurants, from cultural events to sports activities. Boa Vista is the perfect destination for those who want to enjoy the sun, the sea, and the fun.

How to get there
The easiest way to get to Boa Vista is to fly to Boa Vista International Airport, which is located in the capital, Rabil. The airport receives flights from several European and African cities, as well as from other Cape Verdean islands. From the airport, you can take a taxi or a bus to the main tourist hub of Sal Rei, which is about 6 kilometres away. The taxi fare is around 5 euros, and the bus fare is around 0.5 euros. Alternatively, you can rent a car or a scooter at the airport or in the town.

What to do
There are plenty of things to do in and around Boa Vista, depending on your interests and preferences. Some of the most popular activities are:

Live music: Boa Vista is a great place to enjoy live music, especially Cape Verdean music genres like morna, coladeira, and funana. You can find live music in many bars and restaurants, as well as in the main square of Sal Rei, where local bands and singers perform every night. You can also join the locals in dancing and singing along, or just sit back and enjoy the atmosphere.

Nightclubs: Boa Vista is also a great place to party, as it has some of the best nightclubs in Cape Verde. You can find nightclubs that play a mix of local and international music, as well as themed nights and special events. Some of the best nightclubs in Boa Vista are:

Blue Marlin: This is a cozy and friendly bar and nightclub that plays live music and karaoke every night. It also has a pool table, a dart board, and a TV screen. It is located in Sal Rei, near the beach.

Disco Morabeza: This is a lively and popular nightclub that plays a mix of local and international music, as well as themed nights and special events. It also has a large dance floor, a VIP area, and a bar. It is located in Sal Rei, near the pier.

Legends: This is a modern and stylish nightclub that plays a mix of local and international music, as well as themed nights and special events. It also has a large dance floor, a VIP area, and a bar. It is located in Sal Rei, near the main square.

Restaurants: Boa Vista is also a great place to enjoy a variety of cuisines, from local to international, from seafood to vegetarian. You can find restaurants that offer a range of dishes, as well as a range of prices, from budget to luxury. Some of the best restaurants in Boa Vista are:

Sodade di nha Terra: This is a beachfront restaurant that offers a variety of dishes, such as fish, chicken, pasta, and salads. It also has a sun terrace, a sea view, and a live music. It is located in Sal Rei, on the beach.
L' atelier - cap vert: This is a restaurant that offers a fusion of Cape Verdean and French cuisine, such as couscous, crepes, and pastries. It also has a cozy and colorful atmosphere, and a friendly staff. It is located in Sal Rei, near the main square.
D-wine: This is a wine bar and restaurant that offers a variety of dishes, such as tapas, cheese, and meat. It also has a large selection of wines, as well as a live music. It is located in Sal Rei, near the pier.

Where to stay
There are many accommodation options in and around Boa Vista, ranging from budget to luxury. Some of the best places to stay are:

Hotel Estoril e Residence Cardeal: This is a three-star hotel that is located on the beach, offering convenience and comfort. It has simple and clean rooms, with balconies, air conditioning, and free Wi-Fi. It also has a restaurant, a bar, and a pool. The hotel organizes various activities and excursions, such as quad biking, sailing, diving, and turtle watching. The price per night is around 40 euros.

Hotel Riu Karamboa: This is a five-star hotel that is located on the beach, offering luxury and elegance. It has spacious and stylish rooms, with balconies, air conditioning, and free Wi-Fi. It also has a restaurant, a bar, a pool, a gym, and a spa. The hotel organizes various activities and excursions, such as kite surfing, windsurfing, snorkelling, and whale watching. The price per night is around 200 euros.

Casa Boteto: This is a guesthouse that is located near the beach, offering value and charm. It has cozy and colorful rooms, with air conditioning and free Wi-Fi. It also has a shared kitchen, a lounge, and a terrace. The guesthouse organizes various activities and excursions, such as fishing, sailing, diving, and turtle watching. The price per night is around 30 euros.

Santiago

Santiago is the largest and the most populous island in Cape Verde, and it offers a variety of nightlife and entertainment options for all tastes and budgets. You can find everything from cultural, live music to modern nightclubs, from local bars to international restaurants, from historical events to sports activities. Santiago is the perfect destination for those who want to enjoy the culture, the history, and the fun.

How to get there

The easiest way to get to Santiago is to fly to Praia International Airport, which is located in the capital, Praia. The airport receives flights from several European and African cities, as well as from other Cape Verdean islands. From the airport, you can take a taxi or a bus to the main tourist hub of Praia, which is about 5 kilometres away. The taxi fare is around 5 euros, and the bus fare is around 0.5 euros. Alternatively, you can rent a car or a scooter at the airport or in the city.

What to do
There are plenty of things to do in and around Santiago, depending on your interests and preferences. Some of the most popular activities are:

Live music: Santiago is a great place to enjoy live music, especially Cape Verdean music genres like morna, coladeira, and funana. You can find live music in many bars and restaurants, as well as in the main square of Praia, where local bands and singers perform every night. You can also join the locals in dancing and singing along, or just sit back and enjoy the atmosphere.

Nightclubs: Santiago is also a great place to party, as it has some of the best nightclubs in Cape Verde. You can find nightclubs that play a mix of local and international music, as well as themed nights and special events. Some of the best nightclubs in Santiago are:

Kriol Jazz Club: This is a cozy and friendly bar and nightclub that plays live jazz music and karaoke every night. It also has a pool table, a dart board, and a TV screen. It is located in Praia, near the beach.

Zero Hour: This is a lively and popular nightclub that plays a mix of local and international music, as well as themed nights and special events. It also has a large dance floor, a VIP area, and a bar. It is located in Praia, near the pier.

Legends: This is a modern and stylish nightclub that plays a mix of local and international music, as well as themed nights and special events. It also has a large dance floor, a VIP area, and a bar. It is located in Praia, near the main square.

Restaurants: Santiago is also a great place to enjoy a variety of cuisines, from local to international, from seafood to vegetarian. You can find restaurants that offer a range of dishes, as well as a range of prices, from budget to luxury. Some of the best restaurants in Santiago are:

Restaurante Quintal da Musica: This is a cultural and gastronomic center that offers a variety of dishes, such as fish, chicken, pasta, and salads. It also has a sun terrace, a sea view, and a live music. It is located in Praia, on the beach.

L' atelier - cap vert: This is a restaurant that offers a fusion of Cape Verdean and French cuisine, such as couscous, crepes, and pastries. It also has a cozy and colorful atmosphere, and a friendly staff. It is located in Praia, near the main square.

D-wine: This is a wine bar and restaurant that offers a variety of dishes, such as tapas, cheese, and meat. It also has a large selection of wines, as well as a live music. It is located in Praia, near the pier.

Where to stay
There are many accommodation options in and around Santiago, ranging from budget to luxury. Some of the best places to stay are:

Hotel Oasis Praiamar: This is a four-star hotel that is located on the beach, offering stunning views and easy access to the water. It has spacious and comfortable rooms, with balconies, air conditioning, and free Wi-Fi. It also has a restaurant, a bar, a pool, a gym, and a spa. The hotel organizes various activities and excursions, such as fishing, sailing, diving, and golf. The price per night is around 100 euros.

Hotel Pestana Tropico: This is a five-star hotel that is located on the beach, offering luxury and comfort. It has modern and elegant rooms, with balconies, air conditioning, and free Wi-Fi. It also has a restaurant, a bar, a pool, a gym, and a spa. The hotel organizes various activities and excursions, such as kite surfing, windsurfing, snorkelling, and whale watching. The price per night is around 150 euros.

Hotel Santa Maria: This is a three-star hotel that is located near the beach, offering convenience and value. It has cozy and clean rooms, with air conditioning and free Wi-Fi. It also has a restaurant, a bar, and a pool. The hotel organizes various activities and excursions, such as fishing, sailing, diving, and turtle watching. The price per night is around 50 euros.

Sao Vicente

Sao Vicente is the second most populous island in Cape Verde, and it offers a variety of nightlife and entertainment options for all tastes and budgets. You can find everything from cultural, live music to modern nightclubs, from local bars to international restaurants, from historical events to sports activities. Sao Vicente is the perfect destination for those who want to enjoy the culture, the history, and the fun.

How to get there
The easiest way to get to Sao Vicente is to fly to Sao Vicente International Airport, which is located in the capital, Mindelo. The airport receives flights from several Cape Verdean islands, as well as from Praia, the capital of the country. From the airport, you can take a taxi or a bus to the main tourist hub of Mindelo, which is about 10 kilometres away. The taxi fare is around 10 euros, and the bus fare is around 1 euro. Alternatively, you can rent a car or a scooter at the airport or in the city.

What to do
There are plenty of things to do in and around Sao Vicente, depending on your interests and preferences. Some of the most popular activities are:

Live music: Sao Vicente is a great place to enjoy live music, especially Cape Verdean music genres like morna, coladeira, and funana. You can find live music in many bars and restaurants, as well as in the main square of Mindelo, where local bands and singers perform every night. You can also join the locals in dancing and singing along, or just sit back and enjoy the atmosphere.

Nightclubs: Sao Vicente is also a great place to party, as it has some of the best nightclubs in Cape Verde. You can find nightclubs that play a mix of local and international music, as well as themed nights and special events. Some of the best nightclubs in Sao Vicente are:

Caravela: This is a cozy and friendly bar and nightclub that plays live music and karaoke every night. It also has a pool table, a dart board, and a TV screen. It is located in Mindelo, near the beach.

Disco Syrius: This is a lively and popular nightclub that plays a mix of local and international music, as well as themed nights and special events. It also has a large dance floor, a VIP area, and a bar. It is located in Mindelo, near the pier.
Legends: This is a modern and stylish nightclub that plays a mix of local and international music, as well as themed nights and special events. It also has a large dance floor, a VIP area, and a bar. It is located in Mindelo, near the main square.

Restaurants: Sao Vicente is also a great place to enjoy a variety of cuisines, from local to international, from seafood to vegetarian. You can find restaurants that offer a range of dishes, as well as a range of prices, from budget to luxury. Some of the best restaurants in Sao Vicente are:

Restaurante Chez Loutcha: This is a cultural and gastronomic center that offers a variety of dishes, such as fish, chicken, pasta, and salads. It also has a sun terrace, a sea view, and a live music. It is located in Mindelo, on the beach.
L' atelier - cap vert: This is a restaurant that offers a fusion of Cape Verdean and French cuisine, such as couscous, crepes, and pastries. It also has a cozy and colorful atmosphere, and a friendly staff. It is located in Mindelo, near the main square.
D-wine: This is a wine bar and restaurant that offers a variety of dishes, such as tapas, cheese, and meat. It also has a large selection of wines, as well as a live music. It is located in Mindelo, near the pier.

Where to stay
There are many accommodation options in and around Sao Vicente, ranging from budget to luxury. Some of the best places to stay are:

Hotel Oasis Porto Grande: This is a four-star hotel that is located in the city center, offering convenience and comfort. It has spacious and comfortable rooms, with balconies, air conditioning, and free Wi-Fi. It also has a restaurant, a bar, a pool, a gym, and a spa. The hotel organizes various activities and excursions, such as fishing, sailing, diving, and golf. The price per night is around 100 euros.

Hotel Foya Branca: This is a five-star hotel that is located on the beach, offering luxury and elegance. It has modern and stylish rooms, with balconies, air conditioning, and free Wi-Fi. It also has a restaurant, a bar, a pool, a gym, and a spa. The hotel organizes various activities and excursions, such as kite surfing, windsurfing, snorkelling, and whale watching. The price per night is around 150 euros.

Residencial Beleza: This is a guesthouse that is located near the beach, offering value and charm. It has cozy and colorful rooms, with air conditioning and free Wi-Fi. It also has a shared kitchen, a lounge, and a terrace. The guesthouse organizes various activities and excursions, such as fishing, sailing, diving, and turtle watching. The price per night is around 30 euros.

Cultural Heritage Sites

Cape Verde is a diverse and captivating archipelago off the west coast of Africa, offering a range of attractions for travellers of all tastes and budgets. Whether you are looking for sun, sea, sand, culture, adventure, or nature, you will find something to suit your preferences in this island nation. One of the main draws of Cape Verde is its cultural heritage sites, which are places of importance to cultural or natural heritage as described in the UNESCO World Heritage Convention. Cape Verde has one site inscribed on the World Heritage List, and eight sites on the Tentative List, which reflect the rich and varied history and influences of the islands.

In this subchapter, we will explore some of the top cultural heritage sites that Cape Verde has to offer, as well as provide some useful information on how to get there, what to do, and where to stay. Whether you prefer the historical and architectural sites of Cidade Velha and Praia, or the natural and scenic sites of Fogo and Santa Luzia, Cape Verde will surprise and delight you with its cultural heritage sites.

Cidade Velha, Historic Centre of Ribeira Grande

This is the only site in Cape Verde that is inscribed on the World Heritage List, and it is a must-see for any visitor. It is located on the island of Santiago, and it is the oldest European colonial settlement in the tropics. Founded in 1462 by the Portuguese, it was the first stopover for the Atlantic slave trade, and a strategic point for the exploration and colonization of Africa and the Americas. It was also the capital of Cape Verde until 1770, when it was renamed Cidade Velha (Old City) and replaced by Praia. The town features some of the original street layout and impressive remains, such as two churches, a royal fortress, and a pillory square with a 16th-century marble pillar. It is a symbol of Cape Verdean identity, culture, and history.

How to get there

The easiest way to get to Cidade Velha is to fly to Praia International Airport, which is located in the capital, Praia. The airport receives flights from several European and African cities, as well as from other Cape Verdean islands. From the airport, you can take a taxi or a bus to Cidade Velha, which is about 15 kilometers away. The taxi fare is around 10 euros, and the bus fare is around 1 euro. Alternatively, you can rent a car or a scooter at the airport or in the city.

What to do

There are plenty of things to do in and around Cidade Velha, depending on your interests and preferences. Some of the most popular activities are:

Historical and architectural tour: The best way to explore Cidade Velha is to take a guided tour that will show you the main attractions and tell you the stories behind them. You can visit the Nossa Senhora do Rosario Church, the oldest colonial church in the world, the Sao Filipe Fortress, the former seat of the Portuguese governor, the Pelourinho Square, the former site of slave auctions and executions, and the Banana Street, the oldest street in the town. You can also visit the Archaeological Museum, which displays some of the artifacts and relics found in the town.

Cultural and gastronomic tour: Another way to enjoy Cidade Velha is to take a guided tour that will introduce you to the local culture and cuisine. You can visit the Casa da Dona Chiquinha, a traditional house that showcases the Cape Verdean lifestyle, the Fortim de Sao Francisco, a former military fort that hosts cultural events and exhibitions, and the Former Tarrafal Concentration Camp, a former prison that now serves as a memorial and museum. You can also taste some of the local dishes, such as cachupa, a slow-cooked stew of corn, beans, and fish or meat, and grogue, a local rum made from sugar cane.

Nature and adventure tour: If you are looking for some nature and adventure, you can also take a guided tour that will take you to the surrounding areas of Cidade Velha. You can hike to the Monte Cara, a mountain that resembles a human face, and enjoy the panoramic views of the town and the sea. You can also kayak to the Ilheu de Santa Maria, a small island that has a sandy beach and a lighthouse. You can also snorkel or dive in the clear water and see the coral reef and the marine life.

Where to stay
There are not many accommodation options in and around Cidade Velha, as it is a small and historic town. However, you can find some places to stay nearby, such as:

Hotel Pousada da Cidade Velha: This is a three-star hotel that is located in the heart of Cidade Velha, offering convenience and comfort. It has simple and clean rooms, with private bathrooms, hot water, and free Wi-Fi. It also has a restaurant, a bar, and a terrace. The hotel organizes various activities and excursions, such as historical and cultural tours, hiking, and kayaking. The price per night is around 40 euros.

Hotel Oasis Atlantico Praiamar: This is a four-star hotel that is located on the beach, offering stunning views and easy access to the water. It is located in Praia, about 15 kilometres away from Cidade Velha. It has spacious and comfortable rooms, with balconies, air conditioning, and free Wi-Fi. It also has a restaurant, a bar, a pool, a gym, and a spa. The hotel organizes various activities and excursions, such as fishing, sailing, diving, and golf. The price per night is around 100 euros.

Camping: This is a budget option that is available near the town of Cidade Velha, offering adventure and nature. You can pitch your tent on the grass, or rent a tent at the campsite. You can also use the facilities of the campsite, such as the toilets, the showers, and the kitchen. The price per night is around 10 euros.

Santa Luzia, Branco and Raso

These are three small and uninhabited islands that form a complex of protected areas in Cape Verde. They are located between the islands of Sao Vicente and Sao Nicolau, and they are home to some of the rarest and most endangered species of flora and fauna in the country. They are also known for their scenic beauty, with rocky cliffs, sandy beaches, and turquoise waters. They are a paradise for nature lovers, birdwatchers, and adventurers.

How to get there
The easiest way to get to these islands is to take a boat from the island of Sao Vicente, which is the closest and the most accessible. You can find boats that offer regular or charter trips to these islands, depending on the weather and the demand. The boat trip takes about 2 hours, and the price is around 50 euros per person. Alternatively, you can take a boat from the island of Sao Nicolau, which is farther and less accessible. The boat trip takes about 4 hours, and the price is around 100 euros per person.

What to do
There are plenty of things to do in and around these islands, depending on your interests and preferences. Some of the most popular activities are:

Nature and wildlife tour: The best way to explore these islands is to take a guided tour that will show you the main attractions and tell you the stories behind them. You can visit the Santa Luzia Marine Reserve, which is the largest marine protected area in Cape Verde, and see the coral reef and the marine life. You can also visit the Branco and Raso Islets, which are important breeding sites for seabirds, such as the Cape Verde shearwater, the red-billed tropicbird, and the Cape Verde warbler. You can also see the endemic plants and animals, such as the Santa Luzia skink, the Cape Verde giant gecko, and the Cape Verde spur-thighed tortoise.

Hiking and camping: If you are looking for some adventure, you can also hike and camp on these islands, as long as you have the permission and the equipment. You can hike to the highest point of Santa Luzia, which is 395 metres above sea level, and enjoy the panoramic views of the islands and the sea. You can also camp on the beach of Praia Grande, which is the only sandy beach on the island, and enjoy the tranquility and the starry sky.

Snorkelling and diving: If you are looking for some water activities, you can also snorkel or dive in the clear water and see the coral reef and the marine life. You can rent snorkelling or diving equipment at the boat, or join a guided tour to explore the best spots. You can see a variety of fish and coral, as well as turtles, dolphins, and whales if you are lucky.

Where to stay
There are no accommodation options on these islands, as they are uninhabited and protected. However, you can find some places to stay nearby, such as:

Hotel Foya Branca: This is a five-star hotel that is located on the beach, offering luxury and elegance. It is located on the island of Sao Vicente, near the airport and the boat terminal. It has modern and stylish rooms, with balconies, air conditioning, and free Wi-Fi. It also has a restaurant, a bar, a pool, a gym, and a spa. The hotel organizes various activities and excursions, such as kite surfing, windsurfing, snorkelling, and whale watching. The price per night is around 150 euros.

Hotel Oasis Atlantico Belorizonte: This is a four-star hotel that is located on the beach, offering stunning views and easy access to the water. It is located on the island of Sao Nicolau, near the airport and the boat terminal. It has spacious and comfortable rooms, with balconies, air conditioning, and free Wi-Fi. It also has a restaurant, a bar, a pool, a gym, and a spa. The hotel

organizes various activities and excursions, such as fishing, sailing, diving, and golf. The price per night is around 100 euros.
Camping: This is a budget option that is available on the island of Santa Luzia, offering adventure and nature. You can pitch your tent on the grass, or rent a tent at the campsite. You can also use the facilities of the campsite, such as the toilets, the showers, and the kitchen. The price per night is around 10 euros.

Pedra de Lume Salt Works

This is a historical and natural site that is located on the island of Sal. It is a former salt mine that was established in the 18th century by the Portuguese, and it was one of the main sources of income and trade for the island. The salt works are located in an extinct volcanic crater, which is filled with seawater that evaporates and leaves behind salt crystals. The salt works are also known for their therapeutic properties, as the water is very salty and buoyant, and it is said to have healing effects on the skin and the joints. They are a unique and fascinating attraction for visitors.

How to get there
The easiest way to get to the salt works is to take a taxi or a bus from the main tourist hub of Santa Maria, which is about 18 kilometres away. The taxi fare is around 10 euros, and the bus fare is around 1 euro. Alternatively, you can rent a car or a scooter at the airport or in the town.

What to do
There are plenty of things to do in and around the salt works, depending on your interests and preferences. Some of the most popular activities are:

Historical and cultural tour: The best way to explore the salt works is to take a guided tour that will show you the main attractions and tell you the stories behind them. You can visit the old buildings and machinery that were used to extract and process the salt, as well as the museum that displays some of the artifacts and relics from the salt works. You can also learn about the history and the importance of the salt works for the island and the country.

Therapeutic and relaxing tour: Another way to enjoy the salt works is to take a therapeutic and relaxing tour that will allow you to experience the benefits of the salt water. You can swim or float in the salt ponds, which have a salinity of about 27%, and feel the weightlessness and the warmth of the water. You can also apply the salt mud on your skin, which is said to have cleansing and moisturizing effects. You can also relax on the sun loungers, or visit the nearby café, where you can have a drink or a snack, and use the facilities.

Nature and adventure tour: If you are looking for some nature and adventure, you can also take a tour that will take you to the surrounding areas of the salt works. You can hike to the top of the crater, which is 113 metres above sea level, and enjoy the panoramic views of the salt works and the sea. You can also quad bike or horse ride around the crater, and see the different landscapes and vegetation of the island.

Where to stay
There are many accommodation options in and around the salt works, ranging from budget to luxury. Some of the best places to stay are:

Hotel Morabeza: This is a four-star hotel that is located on the beach, offering stunning views and easy access to the water. It is located in Santa Maria, about 18 kilometres away from the salt works. It has spacious and comfortable rooms, with balconies, air conditioning, and free Wi-Fi. It also has a restaurant, a bar, a pool, a gym, and a spa. The hotel organizes various activities and excursions, such as fishing, sailing, diving, and golf. The price per night is around 100 euros.

Oasis Salinas Sea: This is a five-star hotel that is located on the beach, offering luxury and comfort. It is located in Santa Maria, about 18 kilometres away from the salt works. It has modern and elegant rooms, with balconies, air conditioning, and free Wi-Fi. It also has a restaurant, a bar, a pool, a gym, and a spa. The hotel organizes various activities and excursions, such as kite surfing, windsurfing, snorkelling, and whale watching. The price per night is around 150 euros.

Hotel da Luz: This is a three-star hotel that is located near the beach, offering convenience and value. It is located in Santa Maria, about 18 kilometres away from the salt works. It has cozy and clean rooms, with air conditioning and free Wi-Fi. It also has a restaurant, a bar, and a pool. The hotel organizes various activities and excursions, such as fishing, sailing, diving, and turtle watching. The price per night is around 50 euros.

Casa da Dona Chiquinha

This is a historical and cultural site that is located on the island of Santiago, in the town of Cidade Velha. It is a traditional house that showcases the Cape Verdean lifestyle, culture, and history. It was built in the 18th century by Dona Francisca de Figueiredo, also known as Dona Chiquinha, who was a wealthy and influential woman in the town. She hosted many guests and events in her house, such as poets, musicians, and politicians. The house features some of the original furniture, decorations, and objects, as well as a garden, a chapel, and a museum. It is a place of interest for visitors who want to learn more about the Cape Verdean heritage.

How to get there
The easiest way to get to Casa da Dona Chiquinha is to take a taxi or a bus from the main tourist hub of Praia, which is about 15 kilometres away. The taxi fare is around 10 euros, and the bus fare is around 1 euro. Alternatively, you can rent a car or a scooter at the airport or in the city.

What to do
There are plenty of things to do in and around Casa da Dona Chiquinha, depending on your interests and preferences. Some of the most popular activities are:

Historical and cultural tour: The best way to explore Casa da Dona Chiquinha is to take a guided tour that will show you the main attractions and tell you the stories behind them. You can visit the different rooms of the house, such as the living room, the dining room, the bedroom, and the library. You can also see the various objects and artifacts that belong to Dona Chiquinha, such as paintings, books, clothes, and jewelry. You can also visit the garden, which has a variety of plants and flowers, as well as a fountain and a statue. You can also visit the chapel, which has a beautiful altar and a painting of Dona Chiquinha. You can also visit the museum, which displays some of the historical and cultural aspects of Cidade Velha, such as the slave trade, the colonial period, and the independence movement.

Cultural and gastronomic tour: Another way to enjoy Casa da Dona Chiquinha is to take a cultural and gastronomic tour that will introduce you to the local culture and cuisine. You can participate in various workshops and activities, such as cooking, dancing, singing, and storytelling. You can also taste some of the local dishes, such as cachupa, a slow-cooked stew of corn, beans, and fish or meat, and grogue, a local rum made from sugar cane. You can also enjoy some of the local music and entertainment, such as morna, coladeira, and funana, which are typical Cape Verdean music genres.

Where to stay
There are not many accommodation options in and around Casa da Dona Chiquinha, as it is a small and historic town. However, you can find some places to stay nearby, such as:

Hotel Pousada da Cidade Velha: This is a three-star hotel that is located in the heart of Cidade Velha, offering convenience and comfort. It has simple and clean rooms, with private bathrooms, hot water, and free Wi-Fi. It also has a restaurant, a bar, and a terrace. The hotel organizes various activities and excursions, such as historical and cultural tours, hiking, and kayaking. The price per night is around 40 euros.

Hotel Oasis Atlantico Praiamar: This is a four-star hotel that is located on the beach, offering stunning views and easy access to the water. It is located in Praia, about 15 kilometres away from Casa da Dona Chiquinha. It has spacious and comfortable rooms, with balconies, air conditioning, and free Wi-Fi. It also has a restaurant, a bar, a pool, a gym, and a spa. The hotel organizes various activities and excursions, such as fishing, sailing, diving, and golf. The price per night is around 100 euros.

Camping: This is a budget option that is available near the town of Cidade Velha, offering adventure and nature. You can pitch your tent on the grass, or rent a tent at the campsite. You can also use the facilities of the campsite, such as the toilets, the showers, and the kitchen. The price per night is around 10 euros.

Fortim de São Francisco

This is a historical and cultural site that is located on the island of Boa Vista, in the town of Sal Rei. It is a former military fort that was built in the 19th century by the Portuguese, and it was used to defend the island from pirates and invaders. It is also known as the Fort of Duque de Bragança, after the Portuguese prince who ordered its construction. The fort features some of the original walls, towers, and cannons, as well as a museum that displays some of the artifacts and relics from the fort. It is a place of interest for visitors who want to learn more about the Cape Verdean history and culture.

How to get there
The easiest way to get to Fortim de São Francisco is to take a taxi or a bus from the main tourist hub of Sal Rei, which is about 6 kilometres away. The taxi fare is around 5 euros, and the bus fare is around 0.5 euros. Alternatively, you can rent a car or a scooter at the airport or in the town.

What to do
There are plenty of things to do in and around Fortim de São Francisco, depending on your interests and preferences. Some of the most popular activities are:

Historical and cultural tour: The best way to explore Fortim de São Francisco is to take a guided tour that will show you the main attractions and tell you the stories behind them. You can visit the different parts of the fort, such as the walls, the towers, and the cannons. You can also see the various objects and artifacts that belong to the fort, such as weapons, uniforms, and documents. You can also visit the museum, which displays some of the historical and cultural aspects of Boa Vista, such as the slave trade, the colonial period, and the independence movement.

Cultural and gastronomic tour: Another way to enjoy Fortim de São Francisco is to take a cultural and gastronomic tour that will introduce you to the local culture and cuisine. You can participate in various workshops and activities, such as cooking, dancing, singing, and storytelling. You can also taste some of the local dishes, such as buzio, a slow-cooked stew of shellfish and soy sauce, and grogue, a local rum made from sugar cane. You can also enjoy some of the local music and entertainment, such as morna, coladeira, and funana, which are typical Cape Verdean music genres.

Where to stay
There are many accommodation options in and around Fortim de São Francisco, ranging from budget to luxury. Some of the best places to stay are:

Hotel Estoril e Residence Cardeal: This is a three-star hotel that is located on the beach, offering convenience and comfort. It is located in Sal Rei, near the fort. It has simple and clean rooms, with private bathrooms, hot water, and free Wi-Fi. It also has a restaurant, a bar, and a pool. The hotel organizes various activities and excursions, such as quad biking, sailing, diving, and turtle watching. The price per night is around 40 euros.

Hotel Riu Karamboa: This is a five-star hotel that is located on the beach, offering luxury and elegance. It is located in Sal Rei, near the fort. It has spacious and stylish rooms, with balconies, air conditioning, and free Wi-Fi. It also has a restaurant, a bar, a pool, a gym, and a spa. The hotel organizes various activities and excursions, such as kite surfing, windsurfing, snorkelling, and whale watching. The price per night is around 200 euros.

Casa Boteto: This is a guesthouse that is located near the beach, offering value and charm. It is located in Sal Rei, near the fort. It has cozy and colorful rooms, with air conditioning and free Wi-Fi. It also has a shared kitchen, a lounge, and a terrace. The guesthouse organizes various activities and excursions, such as fishing, sailing, diving, and turtle watching. The price per night is around 30 euros.

Enjoying Cape Verde Without Spending a Dime

Cape Verde is a stunning vacation destination that won't break the bank if you plan wisely. With some research and budget-conscious decision-making, it is possible to enjoy the beautiful beaches, breathtaking landscapes, and rich culture of this African archipelago without overspending. In this subchapter, we will provide you with tips and tricks on how to enjoy Cape Verde without spending a dime.

Free attractions and activities

One of the best ways to save money in Cape Verde is to take advantage of the free attractions and activities that the islands have to offer. You can explore the natural wonders, the historical sites, and the cultural events that will enrich your experience and your knowledge. Here are some of the free attractions and activities that you can enjoy in Cape Verde:

Beaches: Cape Verde is blessed with some of the most beautiful and diverse beaches in the world, and you can enjoy them for free. You can swim, sunbathe, relax, or play on the white, black, or golden sand, and admire the turquoise, blue, or green water. You can also see some of the wildlife that inhabits the beaches, such as turtles, crabs, and birds. Some of the best beaches in Cape Verde are Praia de Santa Maria on Sal, Praia de Chaves on Boa Vista, Praia de Tarrafal on Santiago, and Praia Grande on Santa Luzia.

Hiking: Cape Verde is also blessed with some of the most spectacular and varied landscapes in the world, and you can explore them for free by hiking. You can hike to the highest peaks, the deepest valleys, the most remote villages, or the most scenic viewpoints, and enjoy the views, the flora, and the fauna. You can also learn about the geology, the history, and the culture of the islands by hiking. Some of the best hiking trails in Cape Verde are Pico do Fogo on Fogo, Monte Gordo on Sao Nicolau, Ribeira da Torre on Santo Antao, and Monte Cara on Sao Vicente.

Music: Cape Verde is also blessed with some of the most talented and diverse musicians in the world, and you can enjoy them for free by listening to the local music. Music is an integral part of Cape Verdean culture, and it reflects the rich and varied history and influences of the islands. The blend of traditional rhythms and African, European, and Caribbean sounds create a truly magical and diverse musical scene. Cape Verdeans love to celebrate life with music and dance, and you can join them in the bars, clubs, and festivals that showcase the best of Cape Verdean music. Some of the best places to listen to Cape Verdean music are Kriol Jazz Club on Santiago, Blue Marlin on Boa Vista, and Caravela on Sao Vicente.

Budget-friendly accommodation and transportation

Another way to save money in Cape Verde is to choose budget-friendly accommodation and transportation options that will suit your needs and preferences. You can find a variety of accommodation and transportation options that offer convenience, comfort, and value, without compromising your safety or quality. Here are some of the budget-friendly accommodation and transportation options that you can choose in Cape Verde:

Accommodation: Cape Verde has a range of accommodation options, from luxury hotels to budget guesthouses, from beach resorts to mountain lodges, from city apartments to rural cottages. You can find accommodation options that fit your budget, your style, and your location, and that provide you with the amenities and services that you need. Some of the best budget accommodation options in Cape Verde are Hotel da Luz on Sal, Casa Boteto on Boa Vista, Residencial Beleza on Santiago, and Camping on Santa Luzia. You can also use online platforms such as Airbnb, Booking.com, or Hostelworld to find and book your accommodation in advance, and compare prices and reviews.

Transportation: Cape Verde has a range of transportation options, from flights to boats, from buses to taxis, from cars to scooters. You can find transportation options that fit your budget, your time, and your destination, and that provide you with the comfort and safety that you need. Some of the best budget transportation options in Cape Verde are buses, which are cheap and frequent, and cover most of the islands and towns, taxis, which are affordable and convenient, and can be negotiated and shared, and boats, which are scenic and adventurous, and connect most of the islands. You can also use online platforms such as Skyscanner, Rome2rio, or CV Interilhas to find and book your transportation in advance, and compare prices and schedules.

Budget-friendly food and drinks
Another way to save money in Cape Verde is to choose budget-friendly food and drinks options that will satisfy your appetite and your taste buds. You can find a variety of food and drinks options that offer quality, quantity, and diversity, without breaking your wallet. Here are some of the budget-friendly food and drinks options that you can choose in Cape Verde:

Food: Cape Verde has a rich and varied cuisine, influenced by the African, Portuguese, and Brazilian cultures, and based on the local products, such as fish, seafood, corn, beans, and fruits. You can find food options that suit your budget, your diet, and your palate, and that provide you with the nutrients and the flavors that you need. Some of the best budget food options in Cape Verde are cachupa, a slow-cooked stew of corn, beans, and fish or meat, which is the national dish and can be found in most restaurants and markets, buzio, a tasty traditional stew made with shellfish and soy sauce, which is a specialty of Boa Vista, and pastel, a fried pastry filled with cheese, tuna, or meat, which is a popular snack and can be found in most bakeries and street stalls.

Drinks: Cape Verde has a diverse and delicious selection of drinks, both alcoholic and non-alcoholic, that will quench your thirst and refresh your spirit. You can find drinks options that suit your budget, your mood, and your occasion, and that provide you with the hydration and the enjoyment that you need. Some of the best budget drinks options in Cape Verde are grogue, a local rum made from sugar cane, which is the national drink and can be found in most bars and shops, pontche, a sweet and fruity punch made with grogue, honey, and fruits, which is a festive drink and can be found in most parties and celebrations, and coffee, a hot and aromatic beverage made with local beans, which is a daily drink and can be found in most cafés and restaurants.

Travel Essentials

Cape Verde is a beautiful and diverse destination that offers a range of attractions and activities for travellers of all tastes and budgets. However, before you pack your bags and head to this African archipelago, there are some travel essentials that you need to consider and prepare. Here are some of the travel essentials that you should not forget when travelling to Cape Verde:

Passport and visa: To enter Cape Verde, you need a valid passport that has at least six months of validity and one blank page. You also need to pay an airport security fee of 31 euros, which can be done online or on arrival. You do not need a visa if you are staying for up to 30 days as a tourist. However, if you plan to stay longer or for other purposes, you need to apply for a visa at the Cape Verdean Embassy in Paris, France.

Vaccinations and health insurance: There are no compulsory vaccinations for travelling to Cape Verde, but it is recommended to have some routine vaccinations, such as tetanus, diphtheria, hepatitis A, and typhoid. You may also need a yellow fever certificate if you are coming from a country with a risk of yellow fever transmission2. It is also advisable to have a comprehensive health insurance that covers medical expenses, evacuation, and repatriation in case of an emergency. You can also check the TravelHealthPro website for more health advice and updates.

Money and cards: The official currency of Cape Verde is the Cape Verdean escudo (CVE), which is pegged to the euro at a rate of 1 euro = 110.265 CVE. You can exchange money at the airport, banks, hotels, or bureaux de change, but the rates may vary. You can also withdraw money from ATMs, which are widely available in the main towns and islands. However, you may be charged a fee by your bank or the local bank. You can also use credit cards, such as Visa or Mastercard, at some hotels, restaurants, and shops, but they may charge a commission or a surcharge. It is advisable to inform your bank before you travel to Cape Verde and activate your card for Africa. You can also check the exchange rates and fees on the XE website.

Clothing and shoes: Cape Verde has a very dry and sunny climate, with average temperatures ranging from 24°C to 29°C throughout the year. However, the weather can vary depending on the season, the island, and the altitude. Therefore, it is advisable to pack clothing and shoes that are suitable for different conditions and activities. Some of the clothing and shoes that you should pack are:

Light and breathable clothing, such as cotton or linen, that can protect you from the sun and the heat. You can also pack some warmer clothing, such as a sweater or a jacket, for the cooler evenings or the higher altitudes.
Comfortable and sturdy shoes, such as sandals or sneakers, that can handle the different terrains and activities. You can also pack some hiking boots, if you plan to do some trekking or mountain climbing, or some water shoes, if you plan to do some water sports or swimming.
Swimwear and beachwear, such as a swimsuit, a towel, a hat, and sunglasses, that can allow you to enjoy the beautiful beaches and the clear water. You can also pack some sunscreen, aloe vera, and insect repellent, to protect your skin from the sun, the salt, and the bugs.

Cultural and respectful clothing, such as a dress, a skirt, or trousers, that can cover your shoulders and knees, especially when you visit religious or historical sites, or local communities. You can also pack some accessories, such as a scarf, a shawl, or a sarong, that can add some color and style to your outfit.

Gadgets and accessories: Cape Verde has a lot of natural and cultural attractions that you may want to capture and share with your friends and family. Therefore, it is advisable to pack some gadgets and accessories that can enhance your travel experience and memories. Some of the gadgets and accessories that you should pack are:

Camera and charger, such as a digital camera, a smartphone, or a GoPro, that can take high-quality photos and videos of the stunning scenery and the wildlife. You can also pack some extra batteries, memory cards, and a waterproof case, to ensure that you don't miss any shot or moment.

Adapter and power bank, such as a universal adapter, a multi-plug, or a portable charger, that can keep your devices charged and connected. Cape Verde uses the European plug type C, with a standard voltage of 220 V and a frequency of 50 Hz5. You can also check the World Standards website for more information on the plug types and voltages of different countries.

Entertainment and information, such as a laptop, a tablet, or a Kindle, that can provide you with some fun and useful content. You can also download some offline applications and maps, such as Maps.me, Google Translate, or Duolingo, that can help you navigate, communicate, and learn. You can also download some movies, music, or books, that can keep you entertained during your flight or your downtime.

Optimal Times to Visit

Cape Verde is a year-round destination that has something to offer for every traveler. However, depending on your preferences and interests, some times of the year may be more optimal than others. Here are some of the factors that you should consider when choosing the optimal time to visit Cape Verde:

Weather and climate: Cape Verde has a very dry and sunny climate, with average temperatures ranging from 24°C to 29°C throughout the year. However, the weather can vary depending on the season, the island, and the altitude. The dry season runs from November to June, and it is the best time to visit Cape Verde for the weather. The days are warm and sunny, with little or no rain, and the nights are cool and pleasant. The sea temperature is also warm and inviting, averaging around 25°C. The wet season runs from July to October, and it is the least optimal time to visit Cape Verde for the weather. The days are hot and humid, with occasional rain and wind, and the nights are warm and sticky. The sea temperature is also hot and uncomfortable, averaging around 28°C. However, the rain is usually short and heavy, and it brings life and greenery to the islands.

Crowds and prices: Cape Verde is a popular destination that attracts many tourists from different countries and regions. However, depending on the season, the islands may be more or less crowded and expensive. The high season runs from December to March, and it is the least optimal time to visit Cape Verde for the crowds and prices. The islands are busy and bustling, with many visitors coming for the Christmas, New Year, and Easter holidays. The prices are also high and inflated, especially for flights, accommodation, and activities. The low season runs from April to November, and it is the best time to visit Cape Verde for the crowds and prices. The islands are quiet and relaxed, with fewer visitors and more availability. The prices are also low and affordable, especially for flights, accommodation, and activities. However, some facilities and services may be closed or reduced during this time, especially in the rainy season.

Events and festivals: Cape Verde has a rich and diverse culture, influenced by the African, Portuguese, and Brazilian cultures, and it celebrates many events and festivals throughout the year. Depending on your interests and preferences, some times of the year may be more optimal than others to experience the events and festivals. The festive season runs from December to February, and it is the best time to visit Cape Verde for the events and festivals. The islands are lively and festive, with many celebrations and parties for the Christmas, New Year, and Carnival holidays. The Carnival is the biggest and most colorful event in Cape Verde, especially on the island of Sao Vicente, where you can enjoy the music, dance, and costumes of the local people. The cultural season runs from March to November, and it is the least optimal time to visit Cape Verde for the events and festivals. The islands are calm and cultural, with fewer celebrations and parties, but more exhibitions and shows. However, there are still some events and festivals that you can enjoy during this time, such as the Festival of Sao Joao in June, the Festival of Santa Isabel in July, and the Independence Day in July.

Navigating Arrival and Transportation

Cape Verde is a diverse and captivating archipelago off the west coast of Africa, offering a range of attractions and activities for travellers of all tastes and budgets. However, to make the most of your trip, you need to know how to navigate arrival and transportation in Cape Verde. In this subchapter, we will provide you with some useful information and advice on how to get to, from, and around Cape Verde.

Getting to Cape Verde

The easiest and most common way to get to Cape Verde is by plane, as the islands are well connected by air with several European and African cities, as well as with other Cape Verdean islands. Cape Verde has four international airports, located on the islands of Sal, Boa Vista, Santiago, and Sao Vicente. The main airlines that fly to Cape Verde are TAP Air Portugal, Cabo Verde Airlines, Binter Canarias, and TUI Airways.

Depending on your origin and destination, you may need to take a connecting flight or a ferry to reach your final island. For example, if you want to visit Fogo, you need to fly to Santiago first, and then take a domestic flight or a ferry to Fogo. You can check the available routes and schedules on the websites of the airlines and the ferry companies.

Tips and tricks
Book your flights in advance to get the best deals and availability, especially during the high season (December to March).
Check the baggage allowance and fees of your airline, as they may vary depending on the route and the class.

Check the visa and passport requirements of Cape Verde, as they may vary depending on your nationality and the purpose of your visit.

Check the health and safety recommendations of Cape Verde, such as vaccinations, insurance, and precautions.

Check the weather and climate of Cape Verde, as they may vary depending on the season, the island, and the altitude.

Getting from Cape Verde

The easiest and most common way to get from Cape Verde is by plane, as the islands are well connected by air with several European and African cities, as well as with other Cape Verdean islands. Cape Verde has four international airports, located on the islands of Sal, Boa Vista, Santiago, and Sao Vicente. The main airlines that fly from Cape Verde are TAP Air Portugal, Cabo Verde Airlines, Binter Canarias, and TUI Airways.

Depending on your origin and destination, you may need to take a connecting flight or a ferry to reach your departure island. For example, if you are leaving from Fogo, you need to fly or take a ferry to Santiago first, and then take an international flight from there. You can check the available routes and schedules on the websites of the airlines and the ferry companies.

Getting around Cape Verde

The easiest and most common way to get around Cape Verde is by a combination of flights, ferries, buses, and taxis, as the islands have a variety of transportation options that suit different needs and preferences. You can travel between the islands by domestic flights or ferries, and you can travel within the islands by buses, taxis, or rental vehicles. Here are some of the main transportation options that you can use in Cape Verde:

Flights: Cape Verde has seven domestic airports, located on the islands of Sal, Boa Vista, Santiago, Sao Vicente, Sao Nicolau, Fogo, and Maio. The only domestic airline that operates in Cape Verde is BestFly Cabo Verde, which offers regular and charter flights between the islands. The flights are fast and convenient, but they can be expensive and subject to delays or cancellations due to weather or technical issues.

Ferries: Cape Verde has several ferry terminals, located on the islands of Sal, Boa Vista, Santiago, Sao Vicente, Sao Nicolau, Fogo, Maio, Brava, and Santo Antao. The main ferry company that operates in Cape Verde is CV Interilhas, which offers regular and charter ferries between the islands. The ferries are cheap and scenic, but they can be slow and uncomfortable, and subject to delays or cancellations due to weather or technical issues.

Buses: Cape Verde has a network of buses, mostly minibuses or vans, that run on the main roads and connect the main towns and villages on the islands. The buses are locally known as aluguers or yasis, and they operate on a fixed or flexible schedule, depending on the demand and the route. The buses are affordable and frequent, but they can be crowded and cramped, and subject to delays or changes due to traffic or breakdowns.

Taxis: Cape Verde has a fleet of taxis, mostly cars or pick-ups, that run on the main roads and offer door-to-door service on the islands. The taxis are locally known as taxis or hiluxes, and they operate on a metered or negotiated fare, depending on the distance and the route. The taxis are convenient and comfortable, but they can be expensive and scarce, especially during the peak hours or the remote areas.

Rental vehicles: Cape Verde has several rental agencies, mostly local or international, that offer a range of vehicles, such as cars, scooters, quads, or bikes, for rent on the islands. The rental vehicles are available at the airports, the hotels, or the towns, and they require a valid driver's license, a credit card, and a deposit. The rental vehicles are flexible and fun, but they can be costly and risky, especially due to the road conditions, the traffic rules, and the insurance coverage.

Tips and tricks
Plan your transportation in advance to get the best deals and availability, especially during the high season (December to March).
Check the transportation options and prices of your destination, as they may vary depending on the island and the route.
Check the transportation schedule and status of your departure and arrival, as they may change due to weather or technical issues.
Check the transportation safety and quality of your choice, as they may differ due to the vehicle, the driver, and the road conditions.
Check the transportation etiquette and culture of your destination, as they may differ due to the language, the customs, and the expectations.

Essential Travel Tips for a Smooth Journey

Traveling can be an exciting and rewarding experience, but it can also come with some challenges and difficulties. To ensure a smooth and hassle-free journey, it is important to plan ahead and prepare well. Here are some essential travel tips that will help you enjoy your trip and avoid common travel problems.

Research your destination
One of the first steps before traveling is to do some research about your destination. You should learn about the culture, the language, the customs, and the etiquette of the place you are visiting that are provided in this book. You should also find out about the weather, the currency, the transportation, and the safety situation of your destination. This will help you to pack appropriately, communicate effectively, and travel safely.

Check your documents
Another essential step before traveling is to check your documents and make sure they are valid and up-to-date. You should have a valid passport that has at least six months of validity and enough blank pages for stamps and visas. You should also check the visa requirements for your destination and apply for one if needed. You should also have copies of your passport, visa, and other important documents, such as your flight tickets, your hotel reservations, and your travel insurance, in case of loss or theft. You can also scan and email your documents to yourself or store them in a cloud service for easy access.

Pack smart
Packing smart is crucial for a smooth and comfortable journey. You should pack light and only bring the essentials that you need for your trip. You should also pack according to the weather, the activities, and the culture of your destination. You should avoid overpacking or underpacking, as both can cause inconvenience and extra costs. You should also organize your items in a logical and efficient way, using packing cubes, ziplock bags, or compression bags, to save space and time. You should also label your luggage with your name, address, and phone number, and attach a colorful tag or ribbon to make it easy to identify.

Stay healthy
Staying healthy is vital for a smooth and enjoyable journey. You should take care of your health before, during, and after your trip. You should consult your doctor or a travel clinic before your trip and get any necessary vaccinations, medications, or health advice. You should also carry a first-aid kit with some basic supplies, such as bandages, painkillers, antiseptic, and antidiarrheal. You should also practice good hygiene, such as washing your hands, using sanitizer, and avoiding touching your face. You should also eat and drink wisely, avoiding uncooked or unpeeled food, tap water, or ice. You should also stay hydrated, rested, and active, and avoid alcohol, caffeine, or drugs.

Be flexible
Being flexible is key for a smooth and stress-free journey. You should be prepared for any unexpected situations or changes that may occur during your trip, such as flight delays, cancellations, or diversions, bad weather, traffic jams, or strikes. You should also be open to new experiences and opportunities that may arise during your trip, such as meeting new people, trying new food, or exploring new places. You should also have a backup plan in case of emergencies, such as having alternative routes, modes of transportation, or accommodation. You should also have some extra money, time, and patience, and a positive attitude.

Annual Events Calendar

Table

Event	Date	Location
Carnival	February/March (40 days before Easter)	São Vicente (Mindelo)
Kriol Jazz Festival	April	Santiago (Praia)
Baía das Gatas Festival	August (first weekend of the full moon)	São Vicente (Baía das Gatas)
Kavala Fresk Festival	July	São Vicente
Mindelact	November	São Vicente (Mindelo)

10-Day Itineraries for Every Traveler

Beach and Culture Lovers:

If you love relaxing on the beach and exploring the local culture, you can visit the islands of Sal, Boa Vista, and São Vicente. Sal and Boa Vista are known for their stunning beaches, water sports, and desert landscapes. São Vicente is the cultural capital of Cape Verde, where you can enjoy the lively nightlife, music, and art scene. You can also take a day trip to Santo Antão, the greenest and most mountainous island, for some hiking and nature views. A possible itinerary could be:

Day	Island	Activity
1	Sal	Arrive in Sal, check-in, and relax on the beach
2	Sal	Enjoy water sports, such as surfing, kite surfing, or diving
3	Sal	Visit the salt mines of Pedra de Lume and the natural pools of Buracona
4	Boa Vista	Fly to Boa Vista, check-in, and explore the town of Sal Rei
5	Boa Vista	Relax on the beach or join a whale watching or turtle watching tour
6	Boa Vista	Rent a 4x4 or a quad and explore the island's desert and dunes

7	São Vicente	Fly to São Vicente, check-in, and visit the town of Mindelo
8	São Vicente	Take a ferry to Santo Antão and hike in the valleys and mountains
9	São Vicente	Enjoy the cultural activities, such as museums, markets, and live music
10	São Vicente	Depart from São Vicente

Adventure and Nature Lovers:

If you love adventure and nature, you can visit the islands of Santiago, Fogo, and Maio. Santiago is the largest and most populated island, where you can visit the historic capital of Praia, the old fortress of Cidade Velha, and the natural park of Serra Malagueta. Fogo is the most volcanic island, where you can climb the impressive Pico do Fogo and admire the lunar landscape. Maio is the smallest and most tranquil island, where you can enjoy the pristine beaches and the wildlife.

Day	Island	Activity
1	Santiago	Arrive in Santiago, check-in, and visit the city of Praia
2	Santiago	Visit the historic site of Cidade Velha and the fort of São Filipe
3	Santiago	Hike in the natural park of Serra Malagueta and spot the endemic birds
4	Fogo	Fly to Fogo, check-in, and visit the town of São Filipe
5	Fogo	Climb the Pico do Fogo and explore the volcanic crater
6	Fogo	Visit the village of Chã das Caldeiras and taste the local wine and cheese
7	Maio	Fly to Maio, check-in, and relax on the beach

8	Maio	Visit the town of Vila do Maio and the salt flats of Porto Inglês
9	Maio	Join a birdwatching or fishing tour and enjoy the nature
10	Maio	Depart from Maio

Music and Art Lovers:

If you love music and art, you can visit the islands of São Vicente, Santo Antão, and São Nicolau. São Vicente is the birthplace of the famous singer Cesaria Evora and the home of the morna, a genre of Cape Verdean folk music. You can also enjoy the carnival, the jazz festival, and the theater festival that take place on this island. Santo Antão is the greenest and most scenic island, where you can admire the local handicrafts, such as pottery, weaving, and basketry. São Nicolau is a hidden gem, where you can discover the traditional music, dance, and festivals of the island.

Day	Island	Activity
1	São Vicente	Arrive in São Vicente, check-in, and visit the town of Mindelo
2	São Vicente	Enjoy the cultural activities, such as museums, markets, and live music
3	São Vicente	Take a ferry to Santo Antão and hike in the valleys and mountains
4	Santo Antão	Visit the villages of Ponta do Sol, Fontainhas, and Ribeira Grande
5	Santo Antão	Explore the local handicrafts, such as pottery, weaving, and basketry
6	São Nicolau	Fly to São Nicolau, check-in, and visit the town of Ribeira Brava

7	São Nicolau	Discover the traditional music, dance, and festivals of the island
8	São Nicolau	Hike in the natural park of Monte Gordo and spot the endemic plants
9	São Nicolau	Relax on the beach or join a fishing or diving tour
10	São Nicolau	Depart from São Nicolau

Island by Island: A Comprehensive Guide

Santiago: The Heart of Cape Verde

Santiago is the largest and most populous island of Cape Verde, and the one that best reflects the country's diverse history and culture. It is home to the capital city of Praia, where you can find modern amenities, colonial architecture, and lively markets. Santiago is also rich in natural beauty, with stunning beaches, rugged mountains, and verdant valleys. Whether you are looking for history, culture, adventure, or relaxation, Santiago has something for everyone.

In this subchapter, you will discover the best places to visit, things to do, and tips to enjoy your stay in Santiago. You will also learn about the island's history, from its role as a hub of the Atlantic slave trade to its struggle for independence. You will also get a glimpse of the island's vibrant music, dance, and cuisine, which reflect the influences of Africa, Europe, and Brazil.

Best Places to Visit

Santiago has many attractions to offer, from historical sites to natural wonders. Here are some of the best places to visit on the island:

Cidade Velha: The oldest settlement in Cape Verde, and a UNESCO World Heritage Site. Here you can explore the ruins of the former Portuguese capital, such as the Fortaleza Real de São Filipe, the Sé Cathedral, and the Pelourinho. You can also visit the Museu da Resistência, which tells the story of the liberation movement against colonial rule.

Serra Malagueta: The highest mountain range in Santiago, and a national park that protects the island's endemic flora and fauna. You can hike along scenic trails, enjoy panoramic views, and spot rare birds and plants. You can also visit the small villages and farms that dot the landscape, and experience the rural life of the islanders.

Tarrafal: A charming seaside town on the northern coast of Santiago, known for its golden sand beach and crystal clear water. You can swim, snorkel, surf, or relax on the shore, or take a boat trip to the nearby islet of Ilhéu de Santa Maria. You can also visit the infamous Tarrafal Concentration Camp, where political prisoners were held during the colonial era and the dictatorship.

Assomada: The second-largest city in Santiago, and a cultural and commercial center. You can browse the colorful market, where you can find local handicrafts, fruits, vegetables, and spices. You can also visit the Museu da Tabanca, which showcases the island's traditional music and dance, or the Nossa Senhora da Graça church, which dates back to the 18th century.

Best Things to Do

Santiago has many activities to offer, from cultural to adventurous. Here are some of the best things to do on the island:

Listen to morna: Morna is the national music genre of Cape Verde, and Santiago is one of its birthplaces. It is a melancholic and soulful music, influenced by Portuguese fado, African rhythms, and Brazilian modinha. You can listen to morna in bars, restaurants, and festivals, or even join a morna workshop and learn how to play the guitar or the cavaquinho, the typical instruments of morna.

Dance to funaná: Funaná is another popular music genre of Cape Verde, and Santiago is its main origin. It is a fast and energetic music, influenced by African accordion, percussion, and dance. You can dance to funaná in clubs, parties, and carnivals, or even join a funaná class and learn how to move your hips and feet to the beat.

Taste cachupa: Cachupa is the national dish of Cape Verde, and Santiago is one of its best places to try it. It is a hearty stew, made with corn, beans, meat, fish, and vegetables. You can taste cachupa in restaurants, street stalls, and homes, or even join a cachupa cooking class and learn how to make it yourself.

Visit the Botanical Garden: The Botanical Garden of São Jorge dos Órgãos is a hidden gem in Santiago, and a must-see for nature lovers. It is a lush oasis, with over 300 species of plants, some of them endemic to Cape Verde. You can visit the Botanical Garden and admire the beauty and diversity of the flora, or even join a guided tour and learn more about the plants and their uses.

Best Tips to Enjoy Your Stay

Santiago is a friendly and welcoming island, but it also has some challenges and peculiarities. Here are some of the best tips to enjoy your stay on the island:

Get a visa: Cape Verde requires a visa for most foreign visitors, and you can apply for it online or on arrival. The visa costs 25 euros and is valid for 30 days. You also need a valid passport, a return ticket, and a proof of accommodation.

Use public transportation: Santiago has a good network of public transportation, including buses, taxis, and aluguers. Buses are cheap and reliable, but they have fixed routes and schedules. Taxis are convenient and comfortable, but they can be expensive and hard to find. Aluguers are shared minibuses or pick-up trucks, that run along the main roads and stop wherever you want. They are fast and cheap, but they can be crowded and noisy.

Learn some Creole: Creole is the native language of Cape Verde, and the most widely spoken on Santiago. It is a mix of Portuguese and African languages, with some variations from island to island. You can learn some Creole phrases and words, such as "olá" (hello), "obrigado" (thank you), and "tudu dretu" (everything is fine). You can also use a phrasebook or a translator app, or ask for help from locals who speak English, French, or Portuguese.

Respect the culture: Santiago has a rich and diverse culture, but it also has some norms and values that you should respect. You should dress modestly, especially in rural areas and religious sites. You should greet people with a handshake, a smile, and a "bom dia" (good morning) or "boa tarde" (good afternoon). You should avoid public displays of affection, especially between same-sex couples. You should also avoid sensitive topics, such as politics, religion, and sexuality.

History of the Island

Santiago has a long and turbulent history, marked by colonization, slavery, and resistance. Here are some of the key events and periods of the island's history:

15th century: Santiago is discovered by Portuguese explorers, who name it Santiago Maior. It is the first island to be colonized by the Portuguese, who establish a settlement in Ribeira Grande, later renamed Cidade Velha. The island becomes a strategic point for the Atlantic slave trade, as well as a target for pirate attacks.

16th century: Santiago is elevated to the status of a city, and becomes the capital of the Portuguese colony of Cape Verde. The island flourishes as a center of commerce, culture, and religion. The island also witnesses the emergence of a Creole identity, as a result of the mixing of Portuguese, African, and other peoples.

17th century: Santiago suffers a decline in its importance and prosperity, due to the rise of other islands, such as São Vicente and São Nicolau, and the competition of other colonial powers, such as the Dutch, the English, and the French. The island also faces frequent droughts, famines, and epidemics, as well as social unrest and rebellions.

18th century: Santiago is devastated by a series of natural disasters, such as earthquakes, volcanic eruptions, and landslides, that destroy many of its buildings and infrastructure. The island also loses its status as the capital of Cape Verde, which is transferred to Praia, a new settlement on the southern coast of the island.

19th century: Santiago experiences a gradual recovery and modernization, thanks to the development of agriculture, industry, and education. The island also benefits from the abolition of slavery, which leads to the emancipation and integration of the enslaved population. The island also witnesses the rise of nationalism and anti-colonialism, inspired by the ideals of the French Revolution and the American War of Independence.

20th century: Santiago plays a pivotal role in the struggle for independence from Portugal, which is led by the African Party for the Independence of Guinea and Cape Verde (PAIGC). The island hosts the headquarters of the PAIGC, as well as the first armed uprising against the colonial regime, in 1959. The island also hosts the proclamation of independence, in 1975, and the establishment of the Republic of Cape Verde, in 1976.

21st century: Santiago continues to be the political, economic, and cultural hub of Cape Verde, as well as the most populous and diverse island of the archipelago. The island faces new challenges and opportunities, such as poverty, inequality, migration, climate change, tourism, and globalization.

Culture of the Island

Santiago has a rich and diverse culture, that reflects the influences of Africa, Europe, and Brazil. Here are some of the aspects and expressions of the island's culture:

Music: Santiago is the birthplace of some of the most popular music genres of Cape Verde, such as morna, funaná, and batuque. Morna is a melancholic and soulful music, influenced by Portuguese fado, African rhythms, and Brazilian modinha. Funaná is a fast and energetic music, influenced by African accordion, percussion, and dance. Batuque is a traditional music, performed by women who sing and clap, while one of them plays a cloth-covered drum. Santiago has also produced some of the most famous musicians of Cape Verde, such as Cesária Évora, the "Barefoot Diva" of morna, and Ildo Lobo, the "Golden Voice" of funaná.

Dance: Santiago is the origin of some of the most popular dance styles of Cape Verde, such as funaná, batuque, and tabanca. Funaná is a fast and energetic dance, that involves moving the hips and feet to the rhythm of the accordion and the ferrinho. Batuque is a traditional dance, that involves forming a circle and taking turns to improvise movements and lyrics. Tabanca is a ritual dance, that commemorates the death and resurrection of Christ, and involves wearing masks, costumes, and bells.

Cuisine: Santiago has a diverse and delicious cuisine, that reflects the influences of Africa, Europe, and Brazil. The island's staple food is cachupa, a hearty stew made with corn, beans, meat, fish, and vegetables. Other typical dishes include xerém, a corn porridge, canja, a chicken soup, and feijoada, a bean and meat stew. The island's specialties include queijo de cabra, a goat cheese, grogue, a sugarcane liquor, and ponche, a fruit punch.

Religion: Santiago has a predominantly Christian population, with about 90% of the islanders belonging to the Roman Catholic Church. The island has many churches, chapels, and shrines, some of them dating back to the colonial era. The island also has a minority of Muslims, Protestants, and followers of African traditional religions, such as Rastafari and Candomblé. The island celebrates many religious festivals, such as Christmas, Easter, and the Feast of the Assumption.

Art: Santiago has a rich and varied artistic expression, that ranges from traditional to contemporary. The island has many craftsmen and women, who create pottery, basketry, embroidery, and jewelry, using local materials and techniques. The island also has many painters, sculptors, and photographers, who depict the island's landscapes, people, and culture, using various media and styles. The island also has many writers, poets, and storytellers, who narrate the island's history, legends, and myths, using various languages and genres.

Sal: A Beach Lover's Paradise

Sal is one of the most popular and touristy islands of Cape Verde, and the one that best suits beach lovers and water sports enthusiasts. It is a flat and arid island, with a long coastline of white sand beaches and turquoise water. It is also a hotspot for windsurfing, kitesurfing, diving, and fishing. Whether you are looking for relaxation, adventure, or entertainment, Sal has something for you.

In this subchapter, you will discover the best places to visit, things to do, and tips to enjoy your stay in Sal. You will also learn about the island's history, from its discovery by Portuguese explorers to its development as a tourist destination. You will also get a glimpse of the island's culture, which is influenced by Africa, Europe, and Brazil.

Best Places to Visit

Sal has many attractions to offer, from natural wonders to cultural landmarks. Here are some of the best places to visit on the island:

Santa Maria: The main town and tourist center of Sal, and the place where most of the hotels, restaurants, bars, and shops are located. Santa Maria has a long and beautiful beach, where you can sunbathe, swim, or enjoy various water sports. Santa Maria also has a lively nightlife, with live music, dancing, and parties.
Pedra de Lume: A former salt mine and a natural attraction, located on the eastern coast of Sal. Pedra de Lume is a crater of an extinct volcano, filled with salt water. You can visit Pedra de Lume and see the salt pans, where the salt is extracted and exported. You can also float in the water, which is said to have therapeutic properties.

Buracona: A natural pool and a geological phenomenon, located on the northern coast of Sal. Buracona is a hole in the volcanic rocks, where the seawater enters and creates a pool. You can visit Buracona and swim in the pool, or admire the "Blue Eye", a spot where the sunlight reflects on the water and creates a blue eye effect.

Espargos: The capital and the administrative center of Sal, and the place where the island's airport is located. Espargos is a small and quiet town, with a few shops, cafes, and restaurants. You can visit Espargos and see the Morro do Coral, a hill that offers a panoramic view of the island. You can also visit the Nossa Senhora das Dores church, which dates back to the 19th century.

Best Things to Do

Sal has many activities to offer, from relaxing to adventurous. Here are some of the best things to do on the island:

Windsurfing: Sal is one of the best places in the world for windsurfing, thanks to its consistent wind, waves, and weather. You can windsurf in various spots on the island, such as Ponta Preta, Ponta Leme, and Kite Beach. You can also join a windsurfing school or a windsurfing tour, and learn from the experts or explore the island by sea.

Kitesurfing: Sal is also one of the best places in the world for kitesurfing, thanks to its strong wind, flat water, and lagoons. You can kitesurf in various spots on the island, such as Kite Beach, Santa Maria Bay, and Shark Bay. You can also join a kitesurfing school or a kitesurfing tour, and learn from the professionals or discover the island by air.

Diving: Sal is a great place for diving, thanks to its clear water, rich marine life, and diverse underwater landscapes. You can dive in various spots on the island, such as Choclassa, Palmeira, and Buracona. You can also join a diving school or a diving tour, and learn from the instructors or visit the best dive sites.

Fishing: Sal is a paradise for fishing, thanks to its abundant fish, such as tuna, marlin, wahoo, and dorado. You can fish in various spots on the island, such as Santa Maria Pier, Palmeira Harbor, and Murdeira Bay. You can also join a fishing school or a fishing tour, and learn from the guides or enjoy a fishing adventure.

Best Tips to Enjoy Your Stay

Sal is a friendly and welcoming island, but it also has some challenges and peculiarities. Here are some of the best tips to enjoy your stay on the island:

Get a visa: Cape Verde requires a visa for most foreign visitors, and you can apply for it online or on arrival. The visa costs 25 euros and is valid for 30 days. You also need a valid passport, a return ticket, and a proof of accommodation.

Use public transportation: Sal has a limited network of public transportation, including buses, taxis, and aluguers. Buses are cheap and reliable, but they have fixed routes and schedules. Taxis are convenient and comfortable, but they can be expensive and hard to find. Aluguers are shared minibuses or pick-up trucks, that run along the main roads and stop wherever you want. They are fast and cheap, but they can be crowded and noisy.

Learn some Creole: Creole is the native language of Cape Verde, and the most widely spoken on Sal. It is a mix of Portuguese and African languages, with some variations from island to island. You can learn some Creole phrases and words, such as "olá" (hello), "obrigado" (thank you), and "tudu dretu" (everything is fine). You can also use a phrasebook or a translator app, or ask for help from locals who speak English, French, or Portuguese.

Respect the culture: Sal has a rich and diverse culture, but it also has some norms and values that you should respect. You should dress modestly, especially in rural areas and religious sites. You should greet people with a handshake, a smile, and a "bom dia" (good morning) or "boa tarde" (good afternoon). You should avoid public displays of affection, especially between same-sex couples. You should also avoid sensitive topics, such as politics, religion, and sexuality.

History of the Island

Sal has a short and recent history, marked by discovery, exploitation, and tourism. Here are some of the key events and periods of the island's history:

15th century: Sal is discovered by Portuguese explorers, who name it Llana, meaning flat. It is the second island to be colonized by the Portuguese, after Santiago. The island is uninhabited and barren, with no fresh water or vegetation.
16th century: Sal is renamed Sal, meaning salt, due to its abundance of salt. The island becomes a source of salt for the Portuguese, who export it to Europe and Africa. The island also becomes a stopover for ships crossing the Atlantic, who replenish their supplies and trade with the locals.
17th century: Sal is neglected by the Portuguese, who focus on other islands, such as São Vicente and São Nicolau, and the competition of other colonial powers, such as the Dutch, the English, and the French. The island remains sparsely populated and underdeveloped, with only a few salt workers and fishermen living there.
18th century: Sal is attacked by pirates, who loot and burn the island's settlements and salt pans. The island also suffers from droughts, famines, and epidemics, that reduce its population and productivity. The island is abandoned by the Portuguese, who leave it to the mercy of nature and fortune.

19th century: Sal is largely ignored by the Portuguese colonial authorities, who focus on other islands with more agricultural and commercial potential. The island remains sparsely populated and underdeveloped, with only a few fishing villages and salt works. The island also suffers from droughts, famines, and diseases, which force many of its inhabitants to emigrate to other countries, especially Brazil.

20th century: Sal undergoes a major transformation, thanks to the development of two sectors: aviation and tourism. In 1939, the Italian airline LATI establishes a stopover in Sal, connecting Europe and South America. In 1942, the British Royal Air Force builds an airfield in Sal, which becomes a strategic base for the Allies during World War II. In 1957, the Portuguese government builds an international airport in Sal, which attracts more airlines and travelers. In 1960, the first hotel is opened in Sal, marking the beginning of the tourism industry. In 1975, Sal becomes part of the independent Republic of Cape Verde, and continues to grow as a tourist destination. In 1999, the island hosts the first edition of the Cape Verde Music Awards, which celebrates the country's musical talent.

21st century: Sal consolidates its position as one of the most popular and touristy islands of Cape Verde, as well as one of the most developed and prosperous. The island attracts millions of visitors every year, who enjoy its beaches, water sports, nightlife, and culture. The island also faces new challenges and opportunities, such as environmental protection, social inclusion, cultural preservation, and economic diversification.

Culture of the Island

Dance: Sal is the origin of some of the most popular dance styles of Cape Verde, such as coladeira, funaná, and kizomba. Coladeira is a romantic and rhythmic dance, that involves moving the hips and arms to the melody of the guitar and the cavaquinho. Funaná is a fast and energetic dance, that involves moving the hips and feet to the rhythm of the accordion and the ferrinho. Kizomba is a sensual and smooth dance, that involves moving the body close to the partner to the beat of the drums and the bass.

Cuisine
Sal has a simple and tasty cuisine, that reflects the influences of Africa, Europe, and Brazil. The island's staple food is fish, which is caught fresh from the sea and cooked in various ways, such as grilled, fried, or stewed. Other typical dishes include cachupa rica, a rich version of the national dish with meat and vegetables, feijoada à brasileira, a bean and meat stew with Brazilian origins, and pastel com diabo dentro, a pastry with a spicy filling. The island's specialties include queijo de cabra, a goat cheese, grogue, a sugarcane liquor, and ponche, a fruit punch.

Religion
Sal has a predominantly Christian population, with about 90% of the islanders belonging to the Roman Catholic Church. The island has many churches, chapels, and shrines, some of them dating back to the colonial era. The island also has a minority of Muslims, Protestants, and followers of African traditional religions, such as Rastafari and Candomblé. The island celebrates many religious festivals, such as Christmas, Easter, and the Feast of the Assumption.

Art
Sal has a modern and varied artistic expression, that ranges from traditional to contemporary. The island has many craftsmen and women, who create pottery, basketry, embroidery, and jewelry, using local materials and techniques. The island also has many

painters, sculptors, and photographers, who depict the island's landscapes, people, and culture, using various media and styles. The island also has many writers, poets, and storytellers, who narrate the island's history, legends, and myths, using various languages and genres.

Boa Vista: The Dunes Island

Boa Vista is one of the most beautiful and desert-like islands of Cape Verde, and the one that attracts many visitors for its dunes, beaches, and wildlife. It is a flat and arid island, with a long coastline of white sand and turquoise water. It is also a windy island, with ideal conditions for surfing, kitesurfing, and windsurfing. Whether you are looking for relaxation, adventure, or entertainment, Boa Vista has something for everyone.

In this subchapter, you will discover the best places to visit, things to do, and tips to enjoy your stay in Boa Vista. You will also learn about the island's history, from its discovery by Portuguese explorers to its development as a tourist destination. You will also get a glimpse of the island's culture, which is influenced by Africa, Europe, and Brazil.

Best Places to Visit

Boa Vista has many attractions to offer, from natural wonders to cultural landmarks. Here are some of the best places to visit on the island:

Sal Rei: The main town and tourist hub of Boa Vista, and the place where most of the hotels, restaurants, bars, and shops are located. Sal Rei has a long and beautiful beach, where you can sunbathe, swim, or join a water sport activity. Sal Rei also has a lively nightlife, with live music, dancing, and parties.

Pedra de Lume: A former salt mine and a natural attraction, located on the eastern coast of Boa Vista. Pedra de Lume is a volcanic crater, filled with salt water, where you can float like in the Dead Sea. You can also visit the old salt works, where you can see the salt pans, the warehouses, and the pier.

Buracona: A natural pool and a geological phenomenon, located on the northern coast of Boa Vista. Buracona is a hole in the lava rocks, where the seawater enters and creates a stunning blue reflection. You can also see the Olho Azul, or the Blue Eye, a smaller hole that looks like an eye when the sun shines through it.

Espargos: The capital and the administrative center of Boa Vista, and the place where the island's airport is located. Espargos is a small and quiet town, with a few shops, cafes, and restaurants. You can also visit the Miradouro, or the viewpoint, where you can enjoy a panoramic view of the island and the ocean.

Best Things to Do

Boa Vista has many activities to offer, from cultural to adventurous. Here are some of the best things to do on the island:

Watch turtles: Boa Vista is one of the most important nesting sites for loggerhead turtles in the world, and you can witness this amazing spectacle from June to October. You can join a guided tour, where you can observe the turtles laying their eggs, hatching, and making their way to the sea. You can also learn more about the conservation efforts and the threats that these endangered animals face.

Ride a quad bike: Boa Vista is a great place to explore by quad bike, as you can drive across the desert, the dunes, and the beaches. You can join a guided tour, where you can visit some of the island's attractions, such as Pedra de Lume, Buracona, and Praia de Chaves. You can also enjoy the thrill and the scenery, as you ride along the dirt roads and the sand tracks.

Visit a pottery workshop: Boa Vista has a tradition of pottery making, and you can learn more about this craft and its history. You can visit a pottery workshop, where you can see how the local artisans use clay, water, and fire to create pots, bowls, and figurines. You can also try your hand at making your own pottery, and take home a souvenir of your experience.

Enjoy a sunset cruise: Boa Vista has a stunning sunset, and you can enjoy it from a different perspective on a boat. You can join a sunset cruise, where you can sail along the coast, admire the views, and watch the sky change colors. You can also relax, listen to music, and have a drink, as you end your day in style.

Best Tips to Enjoy Your Stay

Boa Vista is a friendly and welcoming island, but it also has some challenges and peculiarities. Here are some of the best tips to enjoy your stay on the island:

Get a visa: Cape Verde requires a visa for most foreign visitors, and you can apply for it online or on arrival. The visa costs 25 euros and is valid for 30 days. You also need a valid passport, a return ticket, and a proof of accommodation.

Use public transportation: Boa Vista has a limited network of public transportation, including buses, taxis, and aluguers. Buses are cheap and reliable, but they have fixed routes and schedules. Taxis are convenient and comfortable, but they can be expensive and hard to find. Aluguers are shared minibuses or pick-up trucks, that run along the main roads and stop wherever you want. They are fast and cheap, but they can be crowded and noisy.

Learn some Creole: Creole is the native language of Cape Verde, and the most widely spoken on Boa Vista. It is a mix of Portuguese and African languages, with some variations from island to island. You can learn some Creole phrases and words, such as "olá" (hello), "obrigado" (thank you), and "tudu dretu" (everything is fine). You can also use a phrasebook or a translator app, or ask for help from locals who speak English, French, or Portuguese.

Respect the culture: Boa Vista has a rich and diverse culture, but it also has some norms and values that you should respect. You should dress modestly, especially in rural areas and religious sites. You should greet people with a handshake, a smile, and a "bom dia" (good morning) or "boa tarde" (good afternoon). You should avoid public displays of affection, especially between same-sex couples. You should also avoid sensitive topics, such as politics, religion, and sexuality.

History of the Island

Boa Vista has a short and recent history, marked by discovery, isolation, and tourism. Here are some of the key events and periods of the island's history:

15th century: Boa Vista is discovered by Portuguese explorers, who name it Boa Vista, meaning "good view". It is the third island to be discovered, after Santiago and Fogo. The island is uninhabited and arid, with little vegetation and water. The island is used as a pasture for cattle and goats, brought by the Portuguese settlers from other islands.

16th century: Boa Vista is visited by pirates, privateers, and slave traders, who attack the island and its livestock. The island is also used as a stopover for ships sailing between Europe, Africa, and America. The island remains sparsely populated and underdeveloped, with only a few fishing villages and salt works.

17th century: Boa Vista is colonized by the Portuguese, who establish a settlement in Rabil, on the western coast of the island. The island becomes a center of salt production, exporting salt to Brazil and other countries. The island also witnesses the emergence of a Creole identity, as a result of the mixing of Portuguese, African, and other peoples.

18th century: Boa Vista is elevated to the status of a parish, and becomes part of the municipality of Santiago. The island continues to produce and export salt, as well as other products, such as cotton, hides, and cheese. The island also faces frequent droughts, famines, and epidemics, which reduce its population and prosperity.

19th century: Boa Vista is largely ignored by the Portuguese colonial authorities, who focus on other islands with more agricultural and commercial potential. The island remains sparsely populated and underdeveloped, with only a few fishing villages and salt works. The island also suffers from droughts, famines, and diseases, which force many of its inhabitants to emigrate to other countries, especially Brazil.

20th century: Boa Vista undergoes a major transformation, thanks to the development of the tourism industry. In 1960, the first hotel

is opened in Boa Vista, marking the beginning of the tourist boom. In 1975, Boa Vista becomes part of the independent Republic of Cape Verde, and continues to grow as a tourist destination. In 1998, the island hosts the first edition of the Kite Surf World Cup, which attracts many water sports enthusiasts.
21st century: Boa Vista consolidates its position as one of the most beautiful and touristy islands of Cape Verde, as well as one of the most developed and prosperous. The island attracts millions of visitors every year, who enjoy its dunes, beaches, and wildlife. The island also faces new challenges and opportunities, such as environmental protection, social inclusion, cultural preservation, and economic diversification.

Culture of the Island

Boa Vista has a simple and lively culture, that reflects the influences of Africa, Europe, and Brazil. Here are some of the aspects and expressions of the island's culture:

Music: Boa Vista is the birthplace of some of the most popular music genres of Cape Verde, such as coladeira, funaná, and kizomba. Coladeira is a romantic and rhythmic music, influenced by Portuguese fado, African rhythms, and Brazilian samba. Funaná is a fast and energetic music, influenced by African accordion, percussion, and dance. Kizomba is a sensual and smooth music, influenced by Angolan semba, Caribbean zouk, and French compas. Boa Vista has also produced some of the most famous musicians of Cape Verde, such as Norberto Tavares, the "King of Coladeira", and Lucibela, the "New Voice of Morna".

Dance: Boa Vista is the origin of some of the most popular dance styles of Cape Verde, such as coladeira, funaná, and kizomba. Coladeira is a romantic and rhythmic dance, that involves moving the hips and arms to the melody of the guitar and the cavaquinho. Funaná is a fast and energetic dance, that involves moving the hips and feet to the rhythm of the accordion and the ferrinho. Kizomba is a sensual and smooth dance, that involves moving the body close to the partner to the beat of the drums and the bass.

Cuisine: Boa Vista has a simple and tasty cuisine, that reflects the influences of Africa, Europe, and Brazil. The island's staple food is fish, which is caught fresh from the sea and cooked in various ways, such as grilled, fried, or stewed. Other typical dishes include cachupa rica, a rich version of the national dish with meat and vegetables, feijoada à brasileira, a bean and meat stew with Brazilian origins, and pastel com diabo dentro, a pastry with a spicy filling. The island's specialties include queijo de cabra, a goat cheese, grogue, a sugarcane liquor, and ponche, a fruit punch.

Religion: Boa Vista has a predominantly Christian population, with about 90% of the islanders belonging to the Roman Catholic Church. The island has many churches, chapels, and shrines, some of them dating back to the colonial era. The island also has a minority of Muslims, Protestants, and followers of African traditional religions, such as Rastafari and Candomblé. The island celebrates many religious festivals, such as Christmas, Easter, and the Feast of the Assumption.

Art: Boa Vista has a modern and varied artistic expression, that ranges from traditional to contemporary. The island has many craftsmen and women, who create pottery, basketry, embroidery, and jewelry, using local materials and techniques. The island also has many painters, sculptors, and photographers, who depict the island's landscapes, people, and culture, using various media and styles. The island also has many writers, poets, and storytellers, who narrate the island's history, legends, and myths, using various languages and genres.

Fogo: The Island of Fire

Fogo is one of the most spectacular and dramatic islands of Cape Verde, and the one that best showcases the volcanic origin of the archipelago. It is a round and rugged island, with a huge stratovolcano that dominates its landscape and its climate. It is also a lively and diverse island, with a rich history and culture. Whether you are looking for nature, adventure, or tradition, Fogo has something for everyone.

In this subchapter, you will discover the best places to visit, things to do, and tips to enjoy your stay in Fogo. You will also learn about the island's history, from its discovery by Portuguese explorers to its recent eruptions. You will also get a glimpse of the island's culture, which is influenced by Africa, Europe, and Brazil.

Best Places to Visit

Fogo has many attractions to offer, from natural wonders to cultural landmarks. Here are some of the best places to visit on the island:

Pico do Fogo: The highest peak and the most active volcano of Cape Verde, and the main attraction of Fogo. Pico do Fogo rises to 2,829 metres (9,281 feet) above sea level, and has a large crater with a smaller cone inside. You can hike to the summit, where you can enjoy breathtaking views, or explore the caldera, where you can see the lava flows and the villages of Portela and Bangaeira.

Chã das Caldeiras: The volcanic plateau and the national park of Fogo, and the most unique and scenic area of the island. Chã das Caldeiras is a large depression, surrounded by the walls of the Bordeira, the ancient caldera of the volcano. You can visit the park and admire the beauty and diversity of the flora and fauna, or join a guided tour and learn more about the geology and the ecology of the area.

São Filipe: The capital and the largest town of Fogo, and the place where most of the services and facilities are located. São Filipe is a charming and historic town, with a colonial architecture and a panoramic view of the ocean. You can visit the town and see the old mansions, the churches, and the museums, or join the festivities and the celebrations, such as the Festa de São Filipe, the biggest festival of the island.

Mosteiros: The second-largest town and the agricultural center of Fogo, and the place where most of the crops and the products are grown and produced. Mosteiros is a green and fertile town, with a pleasant climate and a friendly atmosphere. You can visit the town and see the farms, the markets, and the factories, or taste the specialties and the delicacies, such as the cheese, the wine, and the coffee.

Best Things to Do

Fogo has many activities to offer, from cultural to adventurous. Here are some of the best things to do on the island:

Climb the volcano: Climbing the Pico do Fogo is one of the most challenging and rewarding experiences that you can have on Fogo. It is a strenuous and steep hike, that takes about 3-4 hours to reach the summit, and another 2-3 hours to descend. You need a good physical condition, proper equipment, and a local guide to do it. You can also camp on the crater, if you want to spend the night on the volcano.

Explore the caldera: Exploring the Chã das Caldeiras is one of the most fascinating and educational experiences that you can have on Fogo. It is a scenic and varied drive, that takes you through the different landscapes and formations of the volcanic area. You can also stop and visit the villages, the wineries, and the museums, where you can learn more about the history and the culture of the people who live on the volcano.

Enjoy the beach: Enjoying the beach is one of the most relaxing and enjoyable experiences that you can have on Fogo. The island has several beaches, with different characteristics and atmospheres. You can choose from the black sand beach of São Filipe, the white sand beach of Salinas, the rocky beach of Ponta da Salina, or the secluded beach of Curral Velho. You can also swim, snorkel, surf, or fish on the water, or just relax on the shore. Visit a pottery workshop: Visiting a pottery workshop is one of the most authentic and creative experiences that you can have on Fogo. The island has a tradition of pottery making, that dates back to the pre-colonial times. You can visit a pottery workshop, where you can see how the local artisans use clay, water, and fire to create pots, bowls, and figurines. You can also try your hand at making your own pottery, and take home a souvenir of your experience.

Best Tips to Enjoy Your Stay

Fogo is a friendly and welcoming island, but it also has some challenges and peculiarities. Here are some of the best tips to enjoy your stay on the island:

Get a visa: Cape Verde requires a visa for most foreign visitors, and you can apply for it online or on arrival. The visa costs 25 euros and is valid for 30 days. You also need a valid passport, a return ticket, and a proof of accommodation.

Use public transportation: Fogo has a good network of public transportation, including buses, taxis, and aluguers. Buses are cheap and reliable, but they have fixed routes and schedules. Taxis are convenient and comfortable, but they can be expensive and hard to find. Aluguers are shared minibuses or pick-up trucks, that run along the main roads and stop wherever you want. They are fast and cheap, but they can be crowded and noisy.

Learn some Creole: Creole is the native language of Cape Verde, and the most widely spoken on Fogo. It is a mix of Portuguese and African languages, with some variations from island to island. You can learn some Creole phrases and words, such as "olá" (hello), "obrigado" (thank you), and "tudu dretu" (everything is fine). You can also use a phrasebook or a translator app, or ask for help from locals who speak English, French, or Portuguese.

Respect the culture: Fogo has a rich and diverse culture, but it also has some norms and values that you should respect. You should dress modestly, especially in rural areas and religious sites. You should greet people with a handshake, a smile, and a "bom dia" (good morning) or "boa tarde" (good afternoon). You should avoid public displays of affection, especially between same-sex couples. You should also avoid sensitive topics, such as politics, religion, and sexuality.

History of the Island

Fogo has a long and turbulent history, marked by colonization, slavery, and eruptions. Here are some of the key events and periods of the island's history:

15th century: Fogo is discovered by Portuguese explorers, who name it Fogo, meaning "fire". It is the fourth island to be discovered, after Santiago, Fogo, and Maio. The island is uninhabited and volcanic, with a huge cone and a crater. The island is colonized by the Portuguese, who establish a settlement in São Filipe, on the western coast of the island. The island becomes a center of agriculture, commerce, and religion.

16th century: Fogo is visited by pirates, privateers, and slave traders, who attack the island and its inhabitants. The island is also used as a stopover for ships sailing between Europe, Africa, and America. The island flourishes as a center of culture and education, producing some of the most prominent figures of Cape Verde, such as the poet Eugénio Tavares and the priest António Pusich.

17th century: Fogo is elevated to the status of a city, and becomes the capital of the Portuguese colony of Cape Verde. The island continues to produce and export agricultural products, such as sugar, coffee, and wine. The island also witnesses the emergence of a Creole identity, as a result of the mixing of Portuguese, African, and other peoples.

18th century: Fogo suffers a decline in its importance and prosperity, due to the rise of other islands, such as São Vicente and São Nicolau, and the competition of other colonial powers, such as the Dutch, the English, and the French. The island also faces frequent droughts, famines, and epidemics, which reduce its population and wealth.

19th century: Fogo is devastated by a series of natural disasters, such as earthquakes, volcanic eruptions, and landslides, that destroy many of its buildings and infrastructure. The island also loses its status as the capital of Cape Verde, which is transferred to Praia, a new settlement on the southern coast of Santiago. The island also witnesses the rise of nationalism and anti-colonialism, inspired by the ideals of the French Revolution and the American War of Independence.

20th century: Fogo plays a pivotal role in the struggle for independence from Portugal, which is led by the African Party for the Independence of Guinea and Cape Verde (PAIGC). The island hosts the headquarters of the PAIGC, as well as the first armed uprising against the colonial regime, in 1959. The island also hosts the proclamation of independence, in 1975, and the establishment of the Republic of Cape Verde, in 1976 1 The island also experiences several volcanic eruptions, notably in 1951, 1995, and 2014–15 2 The eruptions cause damage and displacement, but also create new land and fertile soil 3

21st century: Fogo continues to be one of the most spectacular and dramatic islands of Cape Verde, as well as one of the most lively and diverse. The island attracts many visitors, who enjoy its nature, adventure, and tradition. The island also faces new challenges and opportunities, such as environmental protection, social inclusion, cultural preservation, and economic diversification

Culture of the Island

Music: Fogo is the origin of some of the most popular music genres of Cape Verde, such as coladeira, funaná, and kizomba. Coladeira is a romantic and rhythmic music, influenced by Portuguese fado, African rhythms, and Brazilian samba. Funaná is a fast and energetic music, influenced by African accordion, percussion, and dance. Kizomba is a sensual and smooth music, influenced by Angolan semba, Caribbean zouk, and French compas. Fogo has also produced some of the most famous musicians of Cape Verde, such as Cesária Évora, the "Barefoot Diva" of morna, and Ildo Lobo, the "Golden Voice" of funaná1

Dance: Fogo is the origin of some of the most popular dance styles of Cape Verde, such as coladeira, funaná, and kizomba. Coladeira is a romantic and rhythmic dance, that involves moving the hips and arms to the melody of the guitar and the cavaquinho. Funaná is a fast and energetic dance, that involves moving the hips and feet to the rhythm of the accordion and the ferrinho. Kizomba is a sensual and smooth dance, that involves moving the body close to the partner to the beat of the drums and the bass2

Cuisine: Fogo has a diverse and delicious cuisine, that reflects the influences of Africa, Europe, and Brazil. The island's staple food is cachupa, a hearty stew made with corn, beans, meat, fish, and vegetables. Other typical dishes include xerém, a corn porridge, canja, a chicken soup, and feijoada, a bean and meat stew. The island's specialties include queijo de cabra, a goat cheese, grogue, a sugarcane liquor, and ponche, a fruit punch3

Religion: Fogo has a predominantly Christian population, with about 90% of the islanders belonging to the Roman Catholic Church. The island has many churches, chapels, and shrines, some of them dating back to the colonial era. The island also has a minority of Muslims, Protestants, and followers of African traditional religions, such as Rastafari and Candomblé. The island celebrates many religious festivals, such as Christmas, Easter, and the Feast of the Assumption4

Art: Fogo has a rich and varied artistic expression, that ranges from traditional to contemporary. The island has many craftsmen and women, who create pottery, basketry, embroidery, and jewelry, using local materials and techniques. The island also has many painters, sculptors, and photographers, who depict the island's landscapes, people, and culture, using various media and styles. The island also has many writers, poets, and storytellers, who narrate the island's history, legends, and myths, using various languages and genres

São Vicente: The Cultural Hub

São Vicente is one of the most vibrant and cosmopolitan islands of Cape Verde, and the one that best showcases the country's cultural diversity and creativity. It is a small and flat island, with a large natural harbour and a dry climate. It is also a lively and dynamic island, with a bustling city and a thriving arts scene. Whether you are looking for history, culture, or entertainment, São Vicente has something for everyone.

In this subchapter, you will discover the best places to visit, things to do, and tips to enjoy your stay in São Vicente. You will also learn about the island's history, from its discovery by Portuguese explorers to its development as a port city and a cultural hub. You will also get a glimpse of the island's culture, which is influenced by Africa, Europe, and Brazil.

Best Places to Visit

São Vicente has many attractions to offer, from natural wonders to cultural landmarks. Here are some of the best places to visit on the island:

Mindelo: The capital and the largest city of São Vicente, and the place where most of the services and facilities are located. Mindelo is a charming and historic city, with a colonial architecture and a panoramic view of the bay. You can visit the city and see the old mansions, the churches, and the museums, or join the festivities and the celebrations, such as the Carnival, the biggest festival of the island.

Laginha: The main beach and the leisure area of Mindelo, and the place where most of the locals and tourists go to relax and have fun. Laginha is a long and beautiful beach, where you can sunbathe, swim, or join a water sport activity. Laginha also has a lively nightlife, with live music, dancing, and parties.

Monte Verde: The highest peak and the most scenic point of São Vicente, and the place where you can enjoy a panoramic view of the island and the ocean. Monte Verde rises to 774 metres (2,539 feet) above sea level, and has a green and lush vegetation. You can hike to the summit, where you can admire the views, or explore the park, where you can see the flora and fauna.

Baía das Gatas: A natural lagoon and a popular beach, located on the northeastern coast of São Vicente. Baía das Gatas is a calm and shallow lagoon, where you can swim, snorkel, or fish. You can also visit the beach, where you can relax, or join the festival, which is one of the largest music events of Cape Verde.

Best Things to Do

São Vicente has many activities to offer, from cultural to adventurous. Here are some of the best things to do on the island:

Listen to morna: Morna is the national music genre of Cape Verde, and São Vicente is one of its birthplaces. It is a melancholic and soulful music, influenced by Portuguese fado, African rhythms, and Brazilian modinha. You can listen to morna in bars, restaurants, and festivals, or even join a morna workshop and learn how to play the guitar or the cavaquinho, the typical instruments of morna.

Dance to coladeira: Coladeira is another popular music genre of Cape Verde, and São Vicente is its main origin. It is a romantic and rhythmic music, influenced by Portuguese fado, African rhythms, and Brazilian samba. You can dance to coladeira in clubs, parties, and carnivals, or even join a coladeira class and learn how to move your hips and arms to the beat.

Taste catchupa: Catchupa is the national dish of Cape Verde, and São Vicente is one of its best places to try it. It is a hearty stew, made with corn, beans, meat, fish, and vegetables. You can taste catchupa in restaurants, street stalls, and homes, or even join a catchupa cooking class and learn how to make it yourself.

Visit the cultural centre: The cultural centre of Mindelo is a hidden gem in São Vicente, and a must-see for culture lovers. It is a former customs warehouse, converted into a modern and multifunctional space, where you can find a library, a gallery, a theatre, and a café. You can visit the cultural centre and admire the exhibitions, the performances, and the workshops, or even join a guided tour and learn more about the history and the culture of the island.

Best Tips to Enjoy Your Stay

São Vicente is a friendly and welcoming island, but it also has some challenges and peculiarities. Here are some of the best tips to enjoy your stay on the island:

Get a visa: Cape Verde requires a visa for most foreign visitors, and you can apply for it online or on arrival. The visa costs 25 euros and is valid for 30 days. You also need a valid passport, a return ticket, and a proof of accommodation.

Use public transportation: São Vicente has a good network of public transportation, including buses, taxis, and aluguers. Buses are cheap and reliable, but they have fixed routes and schedules. Taxis are convenient and comfortable, but they can be expensive and hard to find. Aluguers are shared minibuses or pick-up trucks, that run along the main roads and stop wherever you want. They are fast and cheap, but they can be crowded and noisy.

Learn some Creole: Creole is the native language of Cape Verde, and the most widely spoken on São Vicente. It is a mix of Portuguese and African languages, with some variations from island to island. You can learn some Creole phrases and words, such as "olá" (hello), "obrigado" (thank you), and "tudu dretu" (everything is fine). You can also use a phrasebook or a translator app, or ask for help from locals who speak English, French, or Portuguese.

Respect the culture: São Vicente has a rich and diverse culture, but it also has some norms and values that you should respect. You should dress modestly, especially in rural areas and religious sites. You should greet people with a handshake, a smile, and a "bom dia" (good morning) or "boa tarde" (good afternoon). You should avoid public displays of affection, especially between same-sex couples. You should also avoid sensitive topics, such as politics, religion, and sexuality.

History of the Island

São Vicente has a short and recent history, marked by discovery, isolation, and culture. Here are some of the key events and periods of the island's history:

15th century: São Vicente is discovered by Portuguese explorers, who name it São Vicente, meaning "Saint Vincent". It is the ninth island to be discovered, after Santiago, Fogo, Maio, Boa Vista, Santo Antão, São Nicolau, Brava, and Santa Luzia. The island is uninhabited and arid, with little vegetation and water. The island is used as a pasture for cattle and goats, brought by the Portuguese settlers from other islands.
16th century: São Vicente is visited by pirates, privateers, and slave traders, who attack the island and its livestock. The island is also used as a stopover for ships sailing between Europe, Africa, and America. The island remains sparsely populated and underdeveloped, with only a few fishing villages and salt works.
17th century: São Vicente is colonized by the Portuguese, who establish a settlement in Mindelo, on the northern coast of the island. The island becomes a center of salt production, exporting salt to Brazil and other countries. The island also witnesses the emergence of a Creole identity, as a result of the mixing of Portuguese, African, and other peoples.
18th century: São Vicente suffers a decline in its importance and prosperity, due to the rise of other islands, such as São Vicente and São Nicolau, and the competition of other colonial powers, such as the Dutch, the English, and the French. The island also faces frequent droughts, famines, and epidemics, which reduce its population and wealth.
19th century: São Vicente undergoes a major transformation, thanks to the development of two sectors: aviation and culture. In 1838, the British Royal Navy establishes a coaling station in

Mindelo, which becomes a strategic base for the British Empire. In 1879, the first submarine cable is laid between Europe and South America, passing through Mindelo, which becomes a telegraph station. In 1886, the first steamship service is established between Europe and South America, stopping in Mindelo, which becomes a port city. In 1892, the first newspaper is published in Mindelo, marking the beginning of the cultural boom

20th century: São Vicente consolidates its position as one of the most vibrant and cosmopolitan islands of Cape Verde, as well as one of the most cultural and creative. The island attracts many artists, writers, musicians, and intellectuals, who contribute to the development of the Cape Verdean identity and culture. The island also plays a pivotal role in the struggle for independence from Portugal, which is led by the African Party for the Independence of Guinea and Cape Verde (PAIGC). The island hosts the headquarters of the PAIGC, as well as the first armed uprising against the colonial regime, in 1961. The island also hosts the proclamation of independence, in 1975, and the establishment of the Republic of Cape Verde

20th century (continued): The island also hosts the proclamation of independence, in 1975, and the establishment of the Republic of Cape Verde, in 19761 The island also experiences several volcanic eruptions, notably in 1951, 1995, and 2014–152 The eruptions cause damage and displacement, but also create new land and fertile soil

21st century: São Vicente continues to be one of the most vibrant and cosmopolitan islands of Cape Verde, as well as one of the most cultural and creative. The island attracts many visitors, who enjoy its nature, adventure, and tradition. The island also faces new challenges and opportunities, such as environmental protection, social inclusion, cultural preservation, and economic diversification.

Embracing the Culture

The Rhythms of Cape Verdean Music

One of the most distinctive and captivating aspects of Cape Verdean culture is its music. Music is an integral part of the Cape Verdean identity, as it expresses the history, diversity, and creativity of the people. Cape Verdean music is a fusion of influences from Africa, Europe, and Brazil, resulting in a variety of genres, styles, and instruments. Whether you are listening to a melancholic morna, a lively coladeira, or a fiery funaná, you will be enchanted by the rhythms of Cape Verdean music.

In this chapter, we will explore the origins, characteristics, and evolution of some of the most popular Cape Verdean music genres. We will also introduce you to some of the most famous and influential Cape Verdean musicians, who have brought their music to the world stage. We will also share some tips and recommendations on how to enjoy and appreciate Cape Verdean music, whether you are at home or on the islands.

Morna: The Soul of Cape Verde

Morna is the national music genre of Cape Verde, and the one that has gained the most international recognition, thanks to the legendary singer Cesária Évora. Morna is a form of folk music, usually sung in Cape Verdean Creole, accompanied by clarinet, violin, guitar, and cavaquinho. Morna is a melancholic and soulful music, that reflects the emotions and experiences of the Cape Verdean people, such as love, longing, nostalgia, and sadness.

Morna is believed to have originated on the island of Boa Vista, in the 18th century, as a cheerful and festive music. It later evolved into a more somber and refined music, influenced by Portuguese fado, African rhythms, and Brazilian modinha. Morna spread to other islands, especially São Vicente, where it developed further, with the contributions of composers like Eugénio Tavares and B. Leza. Morna reached its peak of popularity in the 20th century, with the emergence of singers like Ildo Lobo, Titina, and Cesária Évora, who became known as the "Barefoot Diva" and the "Queen of Morna".

Morna is a music that touches the heart and the soul of the listeners, and is considered a symbol of Cape Verdean identity and culture. Some of the most famous and beloved morna songs are "Sodade", "Beijo de Saudade", "Mar Azul", and "Petit Pays".

Coladeira: The Joy of Cape Verde

Coladeira is another popular music genre of Cape Verde, and the one that has the most festive and upbeat vibe. Coladeira is a form of dance music, usually sung in Cape Verdean Creole, accompanied by guitar, cavaquinho, accordion, and percussion. Coladeira is a romantic and rhythmic music, that reflects the humor and optimism of the Cape Verdean people, as well as their social and political issues.

Coladeira is believed to have originated on the island of São Vicente, in the 1930s, as a faster and more playful version of morna. It later incorporated elements from other music genres, such as samba, merengue, and zouk. Coladeira spread to other islands, especially Santiago, where it developed a more urban and modern style, with the use of electric instruments and synthesizers. Coladeira reached its peak of popularity in the

1970s and 1980s, with the emergence of bands like Os Tubarões, Simentera, and Finaçon, and singers like Codé di Dona, Manuel de Novas, and Frank Cavaquim.

Coladeira is a music that makes people dance and smile and is considered a symbol of Cape Verdean joy and vitality. Some of the most famous and catchy coladeira songs are "Cabo Verde Manda Mantenha", "Nha Sonho", "Rosa Rosinha", and "Bo Kin Cre".

Savoring the Local Cuisine

The Flavors of Cape Verdean Food

One of the most enjoyable and rewarding aspects of traveling to Cape Verde is savoring its local cuisine. Cape Verdean food is a reflection of the country's history, geography, and culture, as it combines influences from Africa, Europe, and Brazil. Cape Verdean food is also a celebration of the country's diversity, as it varies from island to island, depending on the availability of ingredients and the preferences of the people.

In this chapter, we will explore the origins, characteristics, and variations of some of the most popular Cape Verdean dishes. We will also introduce you to some of the best places to eat, drink, and shop for food in Cape Verde. We will also share some tips and recommendations on how to enjoy and appreciate Cape Verdean food, whether you are a foodie or a novice.

Cachupa: The National Dish of Cape Verde

Cachupa is the most famous and beloved dish of Cape Verde, and is considered the national dish of the country. Cachupa is a stew, prepared using hominy (dried maize kernels preserved with an alkali), beans, sweet potato, cassava, fish or meat (sausage, goat, beef, or chicken), and frequently morcela (blood sausage). Cachupa is a hearty and nutritious dish, that can be eaten for breakfast, lunch, or dinner.

Cachupa is believed to have originated on the island of Boa Vista, in the 18th century, as a food for the poor. It was later adopted and adapted by the other islands, especially Santiago, where it became a staple food. Cachupa is also a symbol of Cape Verdean identity and culture, as it represents the fusion of different influences and the diversity of the country.

Cachupa can be prepared in different ways, depending on the island, the region, and the family. Some of the most common variations are:

Cachupa Rica: A rich version of cachupa, with more meat and vegetables, usually prepared for special occasions or on weekends.
Cachupa Pobre: A simple version of cachupa, with less meat and vegetables, usually prepared for everyday meals or on weekdays.
Cachupa Refogada: A fried version of cachupa, with eggs and onions, usually prepared for breakfast or as a leftover dish.

Pastel com Diabo Dentro: The Devil Inside
Pastel com diabo dentro is a pastry with a spicy filling, and is one of the most popular snacks and appetizers in Cape Verde. Pastel com diabo dentro is a deep-fried pastry, filled with minced meat, onions, garlic, parsley, and chili peppers. The name of the dish

means "pastry with the devil inside", and refers to the spiciness of the filling.

Pastel com diabo dentro is believed to have originated on the island of São Nicolau, in the 19th century, as a variation of the Portuguese pastel de carne. It was later spread to the other islands, especially São Vicente, where it became a common street food. Pastel com diabo dentro is also a symbol of Cape Verdean humor and creativity, as it plays with the contrast between the sweet pastry and the hot filling.

Pastel com diabo dentro can be eaten as a snack, an appetizer, or a main dish, depending on the size and the quantity. It can be accompanied by sauces, such as ketchup, mustard, or mayonnaise, or by drinks, such as beer, wine, or grogue.

Celebrating Festivals and Traditions

The Spirit of Cape Verdean Culture

One of the most exciting and rewarding aspects of traveling to Cape Verde is celebrating its festivals and traditions. Festivals and traditions are an integral part of the Cape Verdean identity, as they express the history, diversity, and creativity of the people. Cape Verdean festivals and traditions are a fusion of influences from Africa, Europe, and Brazil, resulting in a variety of events, rituals, and customs. Whether you are joining a religious procession, a musical carnival, or a gastronomic fair, you will be immersed in the spirit of Cape Verdean culture.

In this chapter, we will explore the origins, characteristics, and variations of some of the most popular Cape Verdean festivals and traditions. We will also introduce you to some of the best places and times to experience them, and show you how to participate and enjoy them. We will also share some tips and recommendations on how to respect and appreciate Cape Verdean culture, whether you are a local or a visitor.

Carnival: The Party of Cape Verde
Carnival is the most famous and beloved festival of Cape Verde, and the one that has gained the most international recognition, thanks to the spectacular celebrations in Mindelo. Carnival is a pre-Lenten festival, usually held in February or March, that involves music, dance, costumes, and parades. Carnival is a festive and colorful event, that reflects the humor and optimism of the Cape Verdean people, as well as their social and political issues.

Carnival is believed to have originated in the 15th century, as a result of the Portuguese colonization and the introduction of Catholicism. It later evolved into a more secular and popular festival, influenced by African, Brazilian, and Caribbean cultures. Carnival spread to all the islands, but the most elaborate and hedonistic celebrations take place in Mindelo, on the island of São Vicente, where it is considered the cultural capital of Cape Verde.

Carnival is a festival that makes people dance and smile, and is considered a symbol of Cape Verdean joy and vitality. Some of the most famous and catchy carnival songs are "Mamãe Eu Quero", "Viva o Carnaval", "Sodade Matadera", and "Carnaval de São Vicente".

Festa de São João: The Fire of Cape Verde

Festa de São João is another popular festival of Cape Verde, and the one that has the most traditional and authentic vibe. Festa de São João is a midsummer festival, held on June 24, that honors Saint John the Baptist, the patron saint of many villages and towns. Festa de São João involves bonfires, processions, folk dances, and street parties. Festa de São João is a religious and cultural event, that reflects the faith and heritage of the Cape Verdean people, as well as their agricultural and fishing activities.

Festa de São João is believed to have originated in the 16th century, as a result of the Portuguese colonization and the spread of Catholicism. It later incorporated elements from other cultures, such as African, Brazilian, and French. Festa de São João is celebrated on all the islands, but the most unique and scenic celebrations take place in Porto Novo, on the island of Santo Antão, where it is known as "Kolá San Jon", and involves a ritual of bathing in the sea and jumping over the bonfires.

Festa de São João is a festival that brings people together and strengthens their bonds, and is considered a symbol of Cape Verdean faith and heritage. Some of the most famous and beautiful festa de São João songs are "Nôs Tradison", "Festa de São João", "Kolá San Jon", and "Fogo de Amor".

Dress and Etiquette: Tips for Respectful Interactions

How to Dress and Behave in Cape Verde

One of the most important and challenging aspects of traveling to a different country is learning how to dress and behave appropriately, according to the local culture and customs. Dress and etiquette are essential for respectful interactions, as they show your awareness and appreciation of the host country's values and norms. Dress and etiquette can also affect your safety and comfort, as well as your ability to communicate and connect with the locals.

In this chapter, we will explore the dress and etiquette tips for traveling to Cape Verde, and show you how to avoid some common mistakes and misunderstandings. We will also share some dos and don'ts, as well as some examples and scenarios, to help you navigate the social and cultural nuances of Cape Verde. We will also share some resources and references, where you can learn more about Cape Verdean culture and customs.

Dress Code: What to Wear and What to Avoid
Cape Verde has a tropical climate, with warm and sunny weather throughout the year. The average temperature is around 25°C (77°F), with little variation between seasons. However, the weather can also vary depending on the island, the altitude, and the wind. Therefore, it is advisable to check the weather forecast before packing and dressing for your trip.

In general, Cape Verdeans dress casually and comfortably, with light and breathable fabrics, such as cotton and linen. However, Cape Verdeans also dress modestly and conservatively, especially in rural areas and religious sites. Therefore, it is advisable to avoid wearing revealing or tight clothing, such as shorts, skirts, tank tops, or bikinis, unless you are at the beach or the pool. It is also advisable to avoid wearing look-alike military fatigues, as they are illegal and disrespectful.

Some of the recommended clothing items to pack and wear in Cape Verde are:

T-shirts, shirts, and blouses: Choose loose and light tops, preferably with sleeves and collars, to protect yourself from the sun and the wind. You can also opt for colorful and patterned tops, to blend in with the local style and culture.

Pants, jeans, and skirts: Choose long and loose bottoms, preferably made of cotton or linen, to keep yourself cool and comfortable. You can also opt for dark and neutral colors, to avoid stains and dirt. You can also wear skirts, as long as they are below the knee and not too tight or transparent.

Dresses and jumpsuits: Choose simple and elegant dresses and jumpsuits, preferably with sleeves and collars, to cover your shoulders and chest. You can also opt for floral and geometric prints, to add some flair and personality to your outfit. You can also wear dresses and jumpsuits, as long as they are below the knee and not too tight or transparent.

Shoes and sandals: Choose comfortable and sturdy shoes and sandals, preferably with closed toes and heels, to protect your feet from the sun, the sand, and the rocks. You can also opt for sneakers, loafers, or flats, to walk around the city or the countryside. You can also wear sandals, as long as they are not too noisy or flashy.

Hats, sunglasses, and sunscreen: Choose wide-brimmed hats, sunglasses, and sunscreen, to protect yourself from the sun and the wind. You can also opt for straw hats, caps, or scarves, to add some style and charm to your look. You can also wear sunglasses, as long as they are not too dark or reflective.

Jackets, sweaters, and shawls: Choose light and warm jackets, sweaters, and shawls, to keep yourself cozy and comfortable during the night or the winter. You can also opt for cardigans, hoodies, or ponchos, to layer over your clothes. You can also wear shawls, as long as they are not too large or colorful.

Practical Information for Travelers

Finding the Perfect Accommodation

One of the most important and challenging aspects of traveling to a different country is finding the perfect accommodation, according to your needs, preferences, and budget. Accommodation is not only a place to sleep and rest, but also a place to experience and enjoy the local culture and lifestyle. Accommodation can also affect your safety and comfort, as well as your access to transportation and attractions.

In this chapter, we will explore the different types of accommodation available in Cape Verde, and show you how to choose the best one for your trip. We will also share some tips and recommendations on how to book and pay for your accommodation, and how to deal with any issues or problems that may arise. We will also share some resources and references, where you can find and compare accommodation options in Cape Verde.

Types of Accommodation: What to Expect and What to Avoid

Cape Verde has a wide range of accommodation options, from luxury resorts and villas, to budget hotels and guest houses, to camping and homestays. Each type of accommodation has its own advantages and disadvantages, depending on your expectations and preferences. Here are some of the most common types of accommodation in Cape Verde, and what to expect and what to avoid from each one:

Resorts and Villas: These are the most expensive and luxurious accommodation options in Cape Verde, usually located on the islands of Sal and Boa Vista, near the beach and the airport. Resorts and villas offer all-inclusive packages, with amenities such as swimming pools, spas, restaurants, bars, and entertainment. Resorts and villas are ideal for travelers who want to relax and enjoy the sun and the sea, without worrying about anything else. However, resorts and villas can also be crowded and noisy, especially during peak seasons and holidays. Resorts and villas can also be isolated and detached from the local culture and community, making it harder to interact and connect with the locals.

Hotels and B&Bs: These are the most common and affordable accommodation options in Cape Verde, usually located in the cities and towns, near the main attractions and services. Hotels and B&Bs offer comfortable and clean rooms, with amenities such as Wi-Fi, air conditioning, and breakfast. Hotels and B&Bs are ideal for travelers who want to explore and experience the local culture and lifestyle, with easy access to transportation and activities. However, hotels and B&Bs can also vary in quality and service, depending on the price and location. Hotels and B&Bs can also be impersonal and generic, making it harder to feel at home and comfortable.

Guest Houses and Hostels: These are the cheapest and simplest accommodation options in Cape Verde, usually located in the rural areas and villages, near the nature and the scenery. Guest houses and hostels offer basic and shared rooms, with amenities such as kitchen, laundry, and common areas. Guest houses and hostels are ideal for travelers who want to adventure and discover the hidden gems of Cape Verde, with a sense of community and authenticity. However, guest houses and hostels can also be uncomfortable and inconvenient, depending on the facilities and hygiene. Guest houses and hostels can also be unsafe and unreliable, making it harder to trust and communicate with the hosts and the guests.

Camping and Homestays: These are the most alternative and adventurous accommodation options in Cape Verde, usually located in the remote and wild areas, near the volcanoes and the forests. Camping and homestays offer unique and immersive experiences, with amenities such as tents, sleeping bags, and local meals. Camping and homestays are ideal for travelers who want to challenge and enrich themselves, with a close contact with nature and the locals. However, camping and homestays can also be risky and demanding, depending on the weather and the conditions. Camping and homestays can also be culturally and personally sensitive, making it harder to respect and appreciate the differences and the similarities.

Health and Safety Guidelines

One of the most essential and challenging aspects of traveling to a different country is staying healthy and safe, according to the local conditions and risks. Health and safety are crucial for a successful and enjoyable trip, as they affect your well-being and comfort, as well as your ability to participate and have fun. Health and safety can also depend on your personal factors, such as your age, health status, and travel style.

In this chapter, we will explore the health and safety guidelines for traveling to Cape Verde, and show you how to prevent and deal with some common issues and problems. We will also share some tips and recommendations on how to prepare and pack for your trip, and how to access and use the local health and safety services. We will also share some resources and references, where you can find and update the health and safety information for Cape Verde.

Health Risks and Recommended Vaccines

Cape Verde has a tropical climate, with warm and sunny weather throughout the year. The average temperature is around 25°C (77°F), with little variation between seasons. However, the weather can also vary depending on the island, the altitude, and the wind. Therefore, it is advisable to check the weather forecast before packing and dressing for your trip.

Cape Verde has a relatively low risk of infectious diseases, compared to other African countries. However, there are still some health risks that you should be aware of and protect yourself from, such as:

Dengue: A viral infection transmitted by mosquitoes, that causes fever, headache, rash, and joint pain. There is no vaccine or specific treatment for dengue, so prevention is the best option. You can prevent dengue by avoiding mosquito bites, using insect repellent, wearing long-sleeved clothing, and sleeping under a mosquito net. Dengue is more common during the rainy season, from August to October

Hepatitis A: A viral infection that affects the liver, that causes fever, nausea, vomiting, and jaundice. Hepatitis A is spread through contaminated food and water, especially shellfish, fruits, and vegetables. You can prevent hepatitis A by getting vaccinated before your trip, and by practicing good hygiene and food safety. Hepatitis A is endemic in Cape Verde, and can occur at any time of the year

Hepatitis B: A viral infection that affects the liver, that causes fever, fatigue, abdominal pain, and jaundice. Hepatitis B is spread through contact with blood or body fluids, especially through sexual intercourse, sharing needles, or getting tattoos or piercings. You can prevent hepatitis B by getting vaccinated before your trip, and by practicing safe sex and avoiding risky behaviors. Hepatitis B is endemic in Cape Verde, and can occur at any time of the year

Typhoid: A bacterial infection that affects the intestines, that causes fever, headache, diarrhea, and abdominal pain. Typhoid is spread through contaminated food and water, especially poultry, eggs, and dairy products. You can prevent typhoid by getting vaccinated before your trip, and by practicing good hygiene and food safety. Typhoid is endemic in Cape Verde, and can occur at any time of the year

Before you travel to Cape Verde, you should consult your doctor or a travel health clinic, at least 8 weeks before your departure, to get the necessary vaccines and medicines for your trip. You should also check the TravelHealthPro website, to get the latest health advice and updates for Cape Verde. You should also make sure that you have a valid travel health insurance, that covers your medical expenses and evacuation in case of an emergency. For first aid guide, you can get Dr. Michael Close First Aid Guide on Amazon

Understanding Local Laws and Customs

How to Respect and Appreciate Cape Verdean Culture

One of the most rewarding and challenging aspects of traveling to a different country is understanding its local laws and customs, according to the local culture and values. Laws and customs are essential for respectful interactions, as they show your awareness and appreciation of the host country's norms and expectations. Laws and customs can also affect your safety and comfort, as well as your ability to communicate and connect with the locals.

In this chapter, we will explore the local laws and customs for traveling to Cape Verde, and show you how to avoid some common mistakes and misunderstandings. We will also share some tips and recommendations on how to prepare and behave for your trip, and how to access and use the local services and facilities. We will also share some resources and references, where you can find and update the laws and customs information for Cape Verde.

Local Laws: What to Follow and What to Avoid
Cape Verde is a democratic and stable country, with a legal system based on the Portuguese civil law. The country respects human rights and freedoms, and has a low crime rate. However, there are still some local laws that you should be aware of and follow, such as:

Visa and Passport: You need a visa and a valid passport to enter and exit Cape Verde, unless you are from a visa-exempt country, such as the European Union, the United States, or Canada. You can apply for a visa online or on arrival, for a fee of 25 euros, and it is valid for 30 days. You also need a return ticket and a proof of accommodation. You should keep a copy of your passport and visa with you at all times, and report any loss or theft to the local authorities

Drugs and Alcohol: You should avoid any involvement with drugs and alcohol, as they are illegal and punishable by law. Possession, use, and trafficking of drugs can result in fines, imprisonment, or deportation. Consumption of alcohol is allowed, but you should drink responsibly and respect the local culture and religion. You should also avoid driving under the influence of alcohol, as it can result in fines, suspension of license, or imprisonment

Weapons and Explosives: You should avoid any involvement with weapons and explosives, as they are illegal and punishable by law. Possession, use, and trafficking of weapons and explosives can result in fines, imprisonment, or deportation. You should also avoid wearing look-alike military fatigues, as they are illegal and disrespectful

Photography and Filming: You should ask for permission before taking photos or videos of people, places, or events, as it can be considered rude or intrusive. You should also respect the privacy and dignity of the locals, and avoid taking photos or videos of sensitive or sacred sites, such as military bases, government buildings, or religious places. You should also avoid using drones, as they can be considered a security threat or a nuisance

Staying Connected: Communication Tips

Cape Verde is a beautiful destination for travelers who want to enjoy its diverse landscapes, culture, and cuisine. However, staying in touch with your loved ones or your work may not be as easy as in other places. Here are some tips to help you communicate effectively in Cape Verde:

Phone: The dialing code for Cape Verde is +238. You can buy a local SIM card from one of the major networks, such as E-plus, O2, or Vodafone1. However, be aware that calls can be expensive, especially to international numbers. You may want to use a calling app or a prepaid card instead. Most of the islands have mobile phone coverage, but it may be spotty in some remote areas.

Internet: If you need to access the internet, you have a few options. Some hotels and resorts offer wireless internet for a fee, but the speed and reliability may vary. You can also find some internet cafés in the main cities and towns, such as Praia, Mindelo, or Sal. Another option is to use a mobile hotspot device or a data plan from your local SIM card provider. However, this may also be costly and subject to network availability

Some Common Portuguese Phrases

Greeting someone:

Good day: Bon dia	Fine, thank you: Muitu ben, obrigadu
Good afternoon: Boa tardi	
Good evening: Bo noiti	And you?: E bu?
How are you?: Modi bu sta?	Nice to meet you: Gostu di konxe-bu

Asking for directions:
Where is…?: Onde ki e…?
How far is it?: E longi?
Can you show me on the map?: Bu podi mostra-m na mapa?

Left: Skerdu
Right: Direitu
Straight ahead: Diretu
Turn: Bira
Stop: Para

Shopping:

How much is this?: Quanto ki e kusta?
Do you have…?: Bu ten…?
I want to buy…: N kre kompra…
Can I try it on?: N podi spermenta?

Do you accept credit cards?: Bu ta aseta karton di kreditu?
Can you give me a discount?: Bu podi da-m un diskontu?

Dining:

A table for two, please: Un mesa pa dos, pur favor
The menu, please: Karta, pur favor
What do you recommend?: Ki ki bu ta rekomenda?

I am vegetarian: N e vejetarianu
I am allergic to…: N ten alerjia a…
The bill, please: Konta, pur favor
Cheers!: Saude!

Emergency:

Help!: Ajuda!
I need a doctor: N presiza di un doutor
I am sick: N sta dodu
I am lost: N sta perdidu

Call the police: Txoma pulisia
Where is the hospital?: Onde ki e ospital?

Cape Verde Today

Leadership and Governance: The Role of the President

Cape Verde is a small island nation in the Atlantic Ocean, with a population of about 550,000 people. It gained its independence from Portugal in 1975, after a long struggle led by the African Party for the Independence of Guinea and Cape Verde (PAIGC). Since then, Cape Verde has been a stable and democratic country, with regular elections and peaceful transfers of power1

The president of Cape Verde is the head of state and the commander-in-chief of the armed forces. The president is elected by popular vote for a five-year term, renewable once. The president appoints the prime minister, who is the head of government and leads the executive branch. The president also appoints the members of the Supreme Court of Justice, the highest judicial authority in the country. The president has the power to veto laws passed by the National Assembly, the unicameral legislature, and to dissolve it in case of a serious political crisis. The president also represents the country in international affairs and can declare a state of emergency or war

The current president of Cape Verde is José Maria Neves, who was elected in October 2021 with 51.7% of the votes. He is a member of the African Party for the Independence of Cape Verde (PAICV), the center-left party that ruled the country for most of its history. Neves served as the prime minister of Cape Verde from 2001 to 2016, and is credited with overseeing the country's economic and social development, as well as strengthening its relations with the European Union and China

Neves' main challenger in the presidential election was Carlos Veiga, who got 42.4% of the votes. He is a member of the Movement for Democracy (MpD), the center-right party that governed the country from 1991 to 2001, and from 2016 to 2021. Veiga was also the prime minister of Cape Verde from 1991 to 2000, and the leader of the opposition from 2016 to 2021. He advocated for more economic liberalization, fiscal discipline, and anti-corruption measures

Neves' victory ended a 10-year hold on the presidency by the MpD, which had won the previous two presidential elections with Jorge Carlos Fonseca, who served from 2011 to 2021. Fonseca was a lawyer and a professor of law, who promoted the rule of law, human rights, and regional integration. He also mediated several political conflicts in the region, such as the 2012 coup in Guinea-Bissau and the 2016 crisis in The Gambia.

Neves' main task as the president is to restore stability to the tourism-driven economy, which was severely hit by the Covid-19 pandemic. Cape Verde relies heavily on tourism, remittances, and foreign aid for its income, and has been facing a recession, a fiscal deficit, and a high debt burden. Neves has pledged to diversify the economy, invest in renewable energy, improve public services, and fight poverty and inequality. He has also vowed to work with the MpD-led government, which won the parliamentary election in April 2021, and to maintain a constructive dialogue with the opposition and civil society

Cape Verde is widely regarded as a model of democracy and development in Africa, and has been praised for its political stability, social cohesion, and human development. However, it also faces many challenges, such as climate change, unemployment, corruption, and security threats. The role of the president is crucial in addressing these issues and leading the country towards a more prosperous and sustainable future.

Economic Insights and Recent Achievements

Cape Verde is a small island nation that relies heavily on tourism, remittances, and foreign aid for its income. Despite its geographical and natural challenges, Cape Verde has achieved significant social and economic progress since its independence from Portugal in 1975. It has been praised for its political stability, democratic governance, and human development. However, it also faces many challenges, such as economic diversification, fiscal sustainability, and climate resilience.

According to the African Development Bank Group1, Cape Verde's real GDP grew by 7.0% in 2021 and 10.5% in 2022, supported by transport, the digital economy, construction, and tourism. Renewable energy (22% of total power supply) also stimulated growth through reduced energy import costs. However, the country's growth prospects are subject to external shocks, such as the Covid-19 pandemic, the Russia-Ukraine conflict, and the potential recession in Europe, which accounts for 80% of its imports. Inflation increased from 1.9% in 2021 to 8.0% in 2022 due to higher food and energy prices. The fiscal deficit was reduced from 7.2% of GDP in 2021 to 4.7% in 2022, thanks to spending efficiency and improved tax collection. Public debt fell from 143.0% of GDP in 2021 to 128.1% of GDP in 2022, reflecting higher nominal GDP growth. The current account deficit narrowed from 12.8% of GDP in 2021 to 7.8% of GDP in 2022, driven by tourism revenue and remittances. The financial sector is stable, adequately capitalized, and liquid.

The African Development Bank Group1 projects that Cape Verde's real GDP will grow by 5.7% in 2023 and 6.2% in 2024, supported by agriculture, energy, the digital economy, and tourism. However, the country needs to address the following priorities to ensure sustainable and inclusive long-term growth: (i) increasing firm-level productivity to generate more and better jobs; (ii) reducing economic fragmentation by lowering transportation costs among islands; and (iii) building economic resilience to climate shocks. The poverty rate, which increased from 31.6% in 2021 to 35.5% in 2022, is expected to fall to 34% in 2023 with the progressive resumption of economic growth.

Recent Achievements

Cape Verde has made remarkable achievements in various fields in recent years, demonstrating its commitment to social and economic development, regional integration, and global cooperation. Some of the notable achievements are:

In July 2023, Cape Verde became the first sub-Saharan country to be certified as malaria-free by the World Health Organization2. This was the result of decades of efforts by the government, health workers, and communities to prevent, diagnose, and treat malaria cases, as well as to strengthen surveillance and response systems. The elimination of malaria has significant benefits for the health, tourism, and economy of the country.

In October 2021, Cape Verde successfully held its presidential election, which was widely regarded as free and fair by international observers[3]. The election marked the peaceful transfer of power from the center-right Movement for Democracy (MpD) to the center-left African Party for the Independence of Cape Verde (PAICV), ending a 10-year hold on the presidency by the MpD. The new president, José Maria Neves, who served as the prime minister from 2001 to 2016, pledged to restore stability to the tourism-driven economy, diversify the economic base, invest in renewable energy, improve public services, and fight poverty and inequality. He also vowed to work with the MpD-led government, which won the parliamentary election in April 2021, and to maintain a constructive dialogue with the opposition and civil society.

In November 2021, Cape Verde hosted the 13th Summit of the Community of Portuguese Language Countries (CPLP), which brought together the heads of state and government of the nine member states and representatives of the associate observers and international organizations[4]. The summit adopted the Mobility Agreement, which facilitates the movement of citizens among the CPLP countries, as well as the Strategic Vision 2030, which defines the priorities and objectives of the organization for the next decade. The summit also elected the new executive secretary of the CPLP, Rui Figueiredo Soares, the former foreign minister of Cape Verde. The summit showcased Cape Verde's role as a bridge between Africa, Europe, and Latin America, and its contribution to the promotion of the Portuguese language, culture, and values.

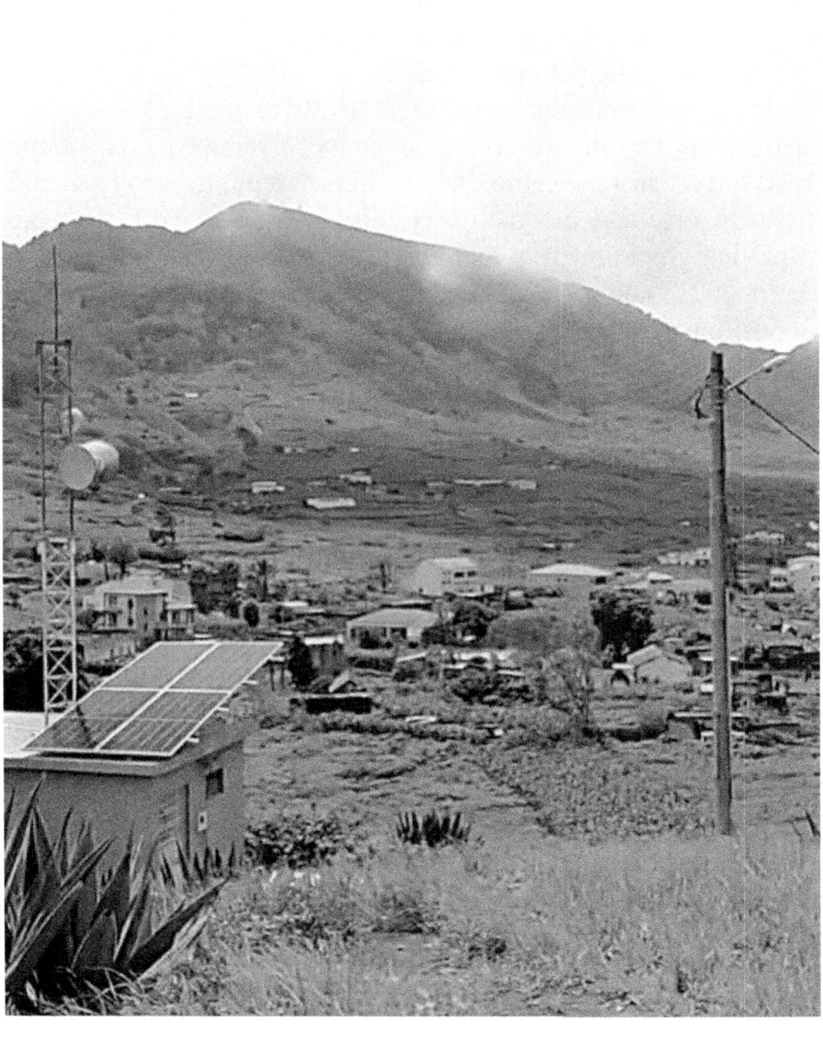

Conclusion

Cape Verde is a destination that offers more than meets the eye. It is not just a collection of islands with stunning beaches and turquoise waters; it is a country with a rich history, a vibrant culture, and a resilient people. Whether you are looking for adventure, relaxation, or inspiration, you will find it in Cape Verde. You will also discover a place that has overcome many challenges and achieved remarkable feats, from eliminating malaria to hosting international summits. Cape Verde is a place that will surprise you, delight you, and transform you. It is a place that will stay with you long after you leave. Thank you for choosing this travel guide book as your companion for your journey to Cape Verde. We hope you have enjoyed reading it as much as we have enjoyed writing it. We wish you a safe and memorable trip. Bon viaje! ☺

Recommendations

When traveling to Cape Verde, there are several apps and websites that can enhance your experience and provide you with valuable information. Here are some recommendations:

1. **Official Cape Verde Tourism Website**: This is the official website for tourism in Cape Verde, offering comprehensive information about the islands, activities, accommodations, and travel tips.

   - Website: www.turismo.cv

2. **Cape Verde Travel Guide by Triposo**: This app provides detailed information about attractions, restaurants, and accommodations in Cape Verde. It also includes offline maps and a currency converter.

   - **App Store:** https://apps.apple.com/us/app/cape-verde-travel-guide/id529463105
   - **Google Play:** https://play.google.com/store/apps/details?id=com.triposo.droidguide.cape_verde&hl=en&gl=US

3. **XE Currency Converter**: Since currency exchange rates can fluctuate, it's useful to have a reliable currency converter app like XE Currency Converter to help you manage your travel budget.

   - Website: www.xe.com
   - App Store: XE Currency & Money Transfers (search name)

- Google Play: XE Currency Converter & Money Transfers (search name)

4. **Google Translate**: Language barriers can sometimes be a challenge, so having a translation app like Google Translate can be very helpful for communicating with locals or understanding signs and menus.

    - Website: translate.google.com
    - App Store: Google Translate (search name)
    - Google Play: Google Translate (search name)

5. **Maps.me**: For accurate and detailed offline maps, Maps.me is a great option. It allows you to download maps of Cape Verde before your trip, so you can navigate the islands without needing an internet connection.

    - Website: maps.me
    - App Store: MAPS.ME: Offline Maps, GPS Nav
    - Google Play: MAPS.ME: Offline maps GPS Nav

6. **Cape Verde Offline Map and Travel Guide**: This app provides an offline map of Cape Verde, along with travel guides and tips for exploring the islands.

    - **App Store:** https://apps.apple.com/us/app/cape-verde-offline-map-and-travel-guide/id1082330658
    - **Google Play:** https://play.google.com/store/apps/details?id=com.offline.maps.capeverde&hl=en&gl=US

Printed in Great Britain
by Amazon